THE
HEBRIDEAN
BAKER

THE
HEBRIDEAN
BAKER

Recipes and Wee Stories
from the Scottish Islands

COINNEACH
MACLEOD

sourcebooks

Published by Sourcebooks
P.O. Box 4410, Naperville, Illinois 60567-4410
(630) 961-3900
sourcebooks.com

Originally published in 2021 in Scotland by Black & White Publishing.

Printed and bound in China

TOP 10 9 8 7 6 5 4 3 2 1

A Phàdruig
Cha b' urrainn dhomh a bhith agus
cha bhithinn air seo a dhèanamh às d' aonais.
'S e sgioba air leth a th' annainn. Mo thaing
chridheil dhut airson creidsinn annam.
Tha gaol agam ort, Coinneach x

CONTENTS

1 – TRADITIONAL BAKES

2 – OATS

3 – BAKES & LOAVES

4 – FROM THE LAND
TO THE SEA

5 – WEE TREATS

6 – CRUMBLES & PUDDINGS

7 – SLÀINTE

8 – FESTIVE BAKES

FÀILTE, I'M THE HEBRIDEAN BAKER

Close your eyes. What is your picture of the Outer Hebrides?

Walking along a deserted beach on a wild, stormy day? Climbing to the top of a heather-strewn hill with a happy wee dog by your side? Sipping a dram of whisky at a cèilidh as a Gaelic song is being sung? Or sitting by your aunt's warm stove waiting for a cake to come out of the oven? For me, it has been all these things, and more . . . and they have inspired every page of this book.

Fàilte, I'm the Hebridean Baker.

My name is Coinneach MacLeod, and I am from the island of Lewis – the furthest north of the Outer Hebrides of Scotland. My love of baking is only equalled by the love I have for the island where I was born – which made writing this cookbook a very special, and humbling, experience. I feel like I am living my dream, sharing recipes and stories from the islands with you. The Hebrides is a larder like no other, with some of the best whisky, seafood, meat and homegrown produce you'll ever be lucky enough to enjoy, and I'm hoping whether you are in Brooklyn, Vancouver or Perth, you'll discover a wee slice of the Hebrides among these pages.

Best of all, I'd love it if this book made you do three things:

1 Come and visit the Hebrides. When the late First Minister of Scotland, Donald Dewar, first visited Lewis, he met an elderly woman working on her croft in Uig on the west coast of the island. He asked her if she felt remote, she lifted her head and said to him: 'Remote from where?' Yes, we might be far away, but we do not feel remote – we are part of a community – and maybe I am biased, but for me, here is the most beautiful place on earth. And, to entice you, I am going to tell you stories about our islands, its culture, language, traditions and legends.

For all of you who travel to the islands, you will go home with a memory you will never forget. Be it standing in the centre of a 5,000-year-old stone circle, hearing the Gaelic language spoken for the first time, unrolling that perfect yard of Harris Tweed, eating the freshest lobster you've ever had, being spun around by a burly man in a kilt at your first cèilidh dance or walking through one of our beautiful villages wondering if your ancestors took the same path. So, now is the time to let YOUR story with the Hebrides begin.

2 Slow down. The Danes created *hygge* – which we can understand as a feeling of contentment. Snuggling up by the fire wrapped in a warm blanket, sipping tea from your favourite mug while a storm rages outside. It is a lifestyle that feels wholesome and nourishing, created from a set of ingredients that include togetherness, presence and comfort.

So, what is the Gaelic word for *hygge*? Well, maybe it's not a direct translation, but the word I would use is *Blàths*, which means warmth, kindliness and contentment. There is a saying in Gaelic '*beiridh blàths air luaths*', it translates as 'there is a time for everything'.

What is my perfect day of *Blàths*? Taking a walk down to the shoreline and hearing the sea roar, looking out the window to see Peter digging in the garden planting his vegetables, pulling all the cookbooks out from the bookshelves and deciding what I'm going to bake, then sitting by the stove learning the tune to an old Gaelic song. Why don't you try it for a day? Maybe *Blàths* could become the way of life you were looking for . . .

3 Try a few of my recipes. My recipes are all wee bakes that use a simple set of ingredients – wholesome and comforting, something you'd serve up when your best friend comes over for a visit. The recipes are rustic, they should taste like a big warm hug (with extra custard!), and when you try one, you really will believe that 'Homemade Is Always Best'. Nothing makes me happier than a day in my kitchen, trying old family recipes, traditional bakes or giving classic recipes my own Scottish twist – which is why, throughout this book, you will find all my favourites. Everything from cranachan, shortbread and clootie dumpling to whisky ice cream, marmalade bread and butter pudding and a couple of cocktails that will be perfect for a burly spin of your own at Hogmanay!

I want to unleash your inner Scottish baker! So go on, turn on the oven, flick through the pages of this book and choose a recipe – they are all delicious, I promise . . .

Coinneach x

COINNEACH'S LARDER

I am passionate about using home-grown Hebridean and Scottish produce. Eating locally first means choosing food that is grown and harvested close to where you live. And each time you do that, you are investing in the local community and its people. Here are some of my favourite producers of quality foods that I use in my kitchen and throughout the recipes in this cookbook. I'd love you to give them a try!

Charles MacLeod Butchers
charlesmacleod.co.uk
For the finest Stornoway Black Pudding and the warmest welcome on the island!

Isle of Harris Distillery
harrisdistillery.com
Not only does Harris Gin come in a beautifully distinctive bottle, it is also flavoured with local, hand-harvested sugar kelp.

Jura Whisky
jurawhisky.com
The wee island of Jura distils my favourite dram; treat yourself to a bottle of their eighteen-year-old whisky for a special occasion.

Hamlyns of Scotland
hamlynsoats.co.uk
I like to start every day with a bowl of porridge. Be it for a traditional warming bowl or overnight oats, I use Hamlyns.

Isle of Skye Sea Salt
isleofskyeseasalt.co.uk
Harvested from the mineral-rich sea waters of Loch Snizort on the Isle of Skye, these pure sea salt crystals have a distinct texture and bring lots of flavour to my savoury dishes.

Golspie Mill
golspiemill.co.uk
Using organic flour in my recipes is important to me. Golspie Mill in Sutherland is one of very few traditional water-powered mills remaining in production in Scotland, and from there they produce my favourite wholemeal flour!

Stag Bakeries
stagbakeries.co.uk
When I'm planning an island picnic, I love popping in to Stag Bakery in Stornoway to grab some treats. Their seaweed biscuits and oatcakes are always in my basket!

Scottish Bee Company
scottishbeecompany.co.uk
Scottish heather honey is produced from bees whose bee-friendly hives are on heather moors in Scotland. No two batches are the same and this smooth sweet honey is perfect for flavouring your tea, porridge and cakes.

HINTS & TIPS

Throughout *The Hebridean Baker* I use certain preparation and baking techniques that I have learned work for me, but you might have your own way that works just as well. And, for example, if you want to add walnuts into my Carrot Cake recipe, then please just do it – I'd love you to put your own twist on my recipes! Here are a few other hints and tips.

When I list the following basics for a recipe, unless stated otherwise, I'd like you to use:
- **Butter.** Unsalted.
- **Eggs.** Medium.
- **Milk.** Whole.
- **Sugar.** Caster.

Most of my ingredients should be readily available. If they aren't, normally there is an easy replacement. For example, you can substitute:
- **Black treacle** with molasses.
- **Bicarbonate of soda** with baking soda.
- **Double cream** with whipping cream.
- **Mixed spice** with pumpkin spice mix.

But, to be honest, golden syrup is unique. If it isn't the core ingredient of the recipe, corn syrup will work, but my recommendation? Hunt for it far and wide, you won't regret it!

You might also prefer these two alternatives:
- **To melt chocolate.** Instead of using a microwave, create a double boiler by bringing a medium pot filled a little less than halfway with water to a simmer. Place a heatproof bowl that's just big enough to sit on top of the pot and add your chocolate. Keep the pot over a low heat and stir with a rubber spatula until silky smooth.
- **Cling film.** Be a planet-friendly baker by replacing cling film with beeswax wraps or reusable silicone food wraps.

Finally, the measurements in this book are in metric. There is a conversion chart below, but can I recommend digital kitchen scales, they are life changing! And while you are in your local kitchen shop, pick up a 1lb loaf tin (450g); I use this size for all my small bakes.

Metric	Imperial
14g	½ oz
28g	1oz
56g	2oz
85g	3oz
100g	3½ oz
453g	1lb
680g	1lb ½ oz
907g	2lb
1kg	2lb 3oz

Metric	Imperial	US
30ml	1fl oz	
60ml	2fl oz	¼ cup
120ml	4fl oz	½ cup
180ml	6fl oz	¾ cup
240ml	8fl oz	1 cup
300ml	10fl oz	1¼ cups
470ml	16fl oz	2 cups/1 US pint
570ml	1 pint	2½ cups
1 litre	1¾ pints	1 quart

VIKINGS & ROOKS

I wonder what it would have been like to have woken up in the Hebrides on the second of July 1266? I would have pulled on my *lèine*, eaten porridge with my family, before heading over the hills to gather my sheep. It would probably have been just another beautiful summer's morning on the island, but this day would go down in history. A few hundred miles away in Perth, a document written in Latin was being signed, meaning I was no longer Norwegian, but Scottish.

The mornings wouldn't be that different for me during my summers growing up on the island in the 1980s. But as my father and brothers would take to the hills, I would climb into our rowing boat on the loch at the end of our croft. I knew the path through the water, avoiding rocks and allowing the tide to take me away from the houses in the village to a wee island. As I got closer, an Iron Age broch loomed above me. This is where my adventures would begin. Dùn Cromore, an Atlantic round-house built 2,000 years before me was my playground.

Many believe it was built as a fort, a place of refuge for the villagers in times of conflict. As I climbed the outer walls, I imagined what it would have been like for the villagers to have seen the Vikings arriving by boats and over hills for the first time. They did not come in peace. In the Heimskringla saga, the Icelandic writer Snorri Sturluson wrote of the adventures of Magnus Barefoot, the King of Norway:

In Lewis Isle with fearful blaze
The house-destroying fire plays;
To hills and rocks the people fly,
Fearing all shelter but the sky.
In Uist the king deep crimson made
The lightning of his glancing blade;
The peasant lost his land and life
Who dared to bide the Norseman's strife.

I always thought that, one day, I would find Viking treasure on the island. A piece of hacksilver in the shape of a brooch or a Viking helmet. But instead, I would pick brambles which grew wild by the stone walls of the broch then row home, imagining how I had kept the village safe from attack for another day. I wonder if these childhood days are the reason that, years later, when I left the island to go to university I chose a degree in Old Icelandic Studies. Maybe it also has something to do with why I call myself the *Beardy Baking Viking from the Outer Hebrides*!

So, after hundreds of years, the Viking settlers began to return home across the northern seas in their skiffs. We were no longer seen as Suðreyjar, the southern isles of Norway, but instead, the Outer Hebrides, the most north-westerly lands of Scotland. In the ninth century, the Vikings arrived on our islands. They named, occupied and managed them and were buried in them for over 450 years. But it was on that date in 1266 that Scotland's King Alexander III agreed to pay King Magnus of Norway the sum of 4,000 merks to secure sovereignty of the Outer Hebrides for Scotland.

By this time, Gaelic and Norse cultures were intertwined and the impact of the Viking era left a lasting mark on the islands, both culturally and linguistically. Those bonds continue to this day. Many Old Norse words were borrowed and adapted by the Gaelic-speakers of the Hebrides to name their villages, hills and islands. These words reflected the importance to both cultures of farming, the sea and the landscape. Of the 126 village names on the island of Lewis, ninety-nine are of purely Old Norse origin.

Habost comes from Old Norse *Hábólstaðr* (High Farm), *Vágr*, which means 'bay', appears in *Stjornavagr*, the word for Steering Bay which became Stornoway. The impact of the sea continues with the beautifully named Salmon Island, *Laxay*, and Herring Point, *Shieldinish*.

But it is not only in the names of our villages, but also in our own family names where you see the Viking influence. In Gaelic, I would introduce myself by saying, *'Hàlo, is mise Coinneach MacLeòid.'* In English, that would be translated as, 'Hello, my name is Kenneth MacLeod.' But, in the thirteenth century, if you'd spoken Old Gaelic and Old West Norse, it would sound like I was introducing myself as, 'Hello, my name is Handsome, Son of Ugly.' Now, my poor father wasn't the best-looking man on the island, but even so, it's a bit harsh! Coinneach derives from the Old Gaelic word *caoin* meaning handsome, *Mac* translates to 'son' and *Leod* comes from the Old Norse *Ljótr*, meaning ugly. What this does mean is that anytime someone shouts 'Hey, ugly!' at me in the street, I smile and wave – wondering, how do they know?

I lived in London during my twenties and, if I was missing home, I would take the underground to Tottenham Court Road and visit the British Museum. I would always get a tingle of excitement as I walked up to the third floor to see the glass case housing The Lewis Chessmen. I would stand there for hours gazing at them, listening to folk stood by me, in awe of the power of this remarkable treasure.

Nearly two hundred years ago, Calum MacLeod was chasing a wayward cow on a beach in Uig on the west coast of Lewis. There in the sand was a wooden box with seventy-eight chess pieces that most likely had been

hidden by a marauding Viking in the twelfth century. Made from walrus ivory and whale teeth, these pieces were probably carved in Trondheim in mid-Norway.

The rooks are my favourite pieces, most commonly known as the Bezerkers. They are depicted as foot soldiers biting their shields. In the Heimskringla saga, it described how the warriors of Óðinn would 'go berserk', entering a frenzied state which involved biting their shields as they went storming into battle.

Calum put them on display in his cow shed in Uig, before selling the whole box of chess pieces for just £30. Maybe he should have held onto them. Recently, in 2019, one of them – a man with helmet, shield and sword, which had been 'lost' in an Edinburgh drawer for years – was sold at auction for just under $1 million.

I don't need to go to London to see the Chessmen anymore, as now, after 150 years off the island, six of the pieces are back in the Outer Hebrides and displayed in the Museum nan Eilean on Lewis. Go and see them when you come and visit.

And when you do visit, take the crossing by ferry. I don't know what it is about getting on a boat, but it always makes me feel that I'm off on an adventure. Much more than a plane or train could ever do. And as you cross over the waters between mainland Scotland and the islands of the Outer Hebrides, it might make

you realise why one of the names the Vikings had for these islands was *Havbredey*, the Old Norse word for 'isles on the edge of the sea'.

Those three or four hours standing out on deck of the Caledonian MacBrayne ferry (usually after a second bowl of their delicious soup!), seeing the waves breaking over the skerries as the mainland disappears behind you, it's impossible not to feel your inner Viking. That you are about to take on a quest, a pilgrimage.

Each island is unique, all have their own identities and idiosyncrasies, not to mention their different landscapes. Just remember that Gaelic saying, *Beiridh blàths air luaths*, there is a time for everything. These are not islands to be rushed. Take your time as you walk along the sands of West Beach on Berneray, pour yourself a hot cuppa from your flask as you look over Stangraidh on the Cromore Walk on the south-east coast of Lewis, or race against the Atlantic waves as you surf off the island of Vatersay. Oh, and did I mention the 5,000-year-old standing stones of Callanish?

Whether you arrive on Barra at the southern pinnacle of the archipelago or Lewis at its most northerly point, I know you will fall in love with these islands. Strewn with its mountains, moors and machair-covered sandy beaches. Just remember to come in peace, we've had more than our fair share of rampaging and pillaging over the years . . .

1
TRADITIONAL BAKES

*Cha bhòrd bòrd gun aran, ach is
bòrd aran leis fhèin*

*A table isn't a table without bread on it
– but bread by itself makes a table.*

SHORTBREAD

(MAKES A DOZEN)

INGREDIENTS

115g soft butter

55g golden caster sugar, plus
extra for sprinkling

Pinch of salt

130g plain flour

40g ground rice

I always buy shortbread at Christmas, not so much for the shortbread itself, but for the wonderfully kitsch tins it comes in, usually adorned with West Highland terriers, stags or cèilidh dances and lots of tartan. Once you've eaten the bought shortbread don't forget to keep the tin to keep your homemade shortbread in instead.

METHOD

Preheat the oven to 150°C/300°F.

Cream together the butter, sugar and salt until pale.

Sift in your flour and ground rice and mix until you make a smooth dough. Cover in cling film and chill in the fridge for 15 minutes.

Lightly roll out the dough to 1cm thickness and cut into biscuits. Sprinkle over the extra sugar.

Bake in the oven for 20 to 25 minutes. Your shortbread pieces should be golden but not browned. Leave to cool on a wire rack.

ORANGE & CLEMENTINE MARMALADE

(MAKES 6 JARS)

INGREDIENTS

2.5 litres water

1 lemon

500g oranges

500g clementines

2kg preserving sugar

This delicious preserve was made famous by Janet Keiller and her son James. After buying the cargo of Seville oranges from a Spanish ship docked in Dundee, Janet boiled them with sugar and Dundee Marmalade was born. Thank you, Janet!

METHOD

Add your water to a large pan.

Cut the lemon, oranges and clementines in half, squeeze out the juice and add to the water. Discard the lemon then remove the fruit, pith and pips from the oranges and clementines and place in a muslin (or a cotton dishtowel) and tie this to the handle of the pan and let it sit in the water.

Cut the peel of the oranges and clementines into shreds – this is when you decide if you want thick cut or thin cut marmalade. Add this to your pan.

Simmer gently, uncovered, for 2 hours. The best way to check if it's ready is to see if you can squeeze a shred of peel in half with a finger and thumb.

Place 1 or 2 small plates or saucers in the freezer – you will need them later!

Remove your bag of fruit, then add your sugar and stir over a low heat until it has dissolved. Once it's a wee bit cooler, squeeze the bag and allow the jelly-like pectin substance to pour into the pan. Stir this all together and then get the pan to a boil for 15 minutes, giving it an occasional stir.

To test if it has set, add a spoonful of the marmalade onto one of the cold plates from the freezer. When it has cooled, push the marmalade with a finger: if it crinkles, it is set. If not, continue to boil the marmalade and give it the same test at about 3-minute intervals until it does set. Leave the marmalade to settle for 10 minutes.

Pour the marmalade into sterilised warm jars and close the lids while still hot. Serve on thick buttery sourdough toast.

AUNT BELLAG'S DUFF

INGREDIENTS

225g plain flour

1 teaspoon baking soda

1 teaspoon mixed spice

1 teaspoon cinnamon

Pinch of salt

175g sugar

100g suet

100g sultanas

75g currants

75g raisins

1 apple, grated

150ml buttermilk

1 egg, beaten

1 heaped tablespoon black treacle

1 heaped tablespoon marmalade (see page 21 to make your own)

Clootie dumpling or *duff* as we say in Gaelic, is my favourite traditional recipe. And no one makes it better than my Aunt Bellag. She adds an extra ingredient, a tablespoon of marmalade – which I love. Its distinctive skin sets it apart from other fruit cakes. Serve this warm with custard, or the next morning fried in bacon fat as part of a Hebridean breakfast. It takes a bit more effort than a lot of my recipes, but it's definitely worth it.

METHOD

Everything goes in a single bowl! Sieve your flour and add your baking soda, mixed spice, cinnamon and salt into a bowl and combine.

Add your sugar, suet, dried fruit and grated apple to the bowl and stir together.

Pour in your buttermilk, beaten egg, black treacle and marmalade. Combine together.

Place a piece of muslin cloth or a cotton dishtowel (the cloot) in boiling water, and once cool enough to touch, wring the cloth out. Place the cloth on your work surface and sprinkle liberally with flour.

Place the mixture into the centre of the cloot. Gather up the edges of the cloth and with a length of string tie it up (not too tightly), leaving some room for the dumpling to expand.

In a large pan of boiling water (deep enough to cover the dumpling), place a saucer upside down. Place the dumpling onto the saucer, cover with a lid and simmer for 3 hours. Don't let the water evaporate; you may need to top it up.

Take out from the pan and carefully remove the cloot from the dumpling, trying not to take off any of the 'skin'. In a warm kitchen, let it rest for 30 minutes before slicing.

DUNDEE MUFFINS

(MAKES A DOZEN)

INGREDIENTS

For the muffins

175g soft butter

175g soft brown sugar

3 tablespoons marmalade
(see page 21 to make
your own)

3 eggs

225g self-raising flour

25g ground almonds

1 heaped teaspoon mixed
spice

400g mixed dried fruit

2 tablespoons whisky

40g blanched almonds

For the glaze

2 tablespoons marmalade

Rumour has it Mary, Queen of Scots did not like glacé cherries in her fruit cake, so this cake with blanched almonds was made for her instead. It's one of the most famous cakes baked in the shop of Janet Keiller in Dundee.

METHOD

Preheat your oven to 180°C/350°F. Line a muffin tin with paper liners.

Cream the butter and soft brown sugar until light. Add the marmalade and mix for a few seconds before slowly adding the eggs.

Add the flour, almonds and spice to the batter. Mix slowly until well combined, then stir in the mixed dried fruit and whisky with a large metal spoon.

Add roughly 2 tablespoons of the batter into each muffin case and create the distinctive Dundee Cake design by arranging the blanched almonds in a circle on top.

Bake for 25 minutes or until a skewer comes out clean. They should be golden brown.

Warm your marmalade for 10 seconds in the microwave or gently in a small pan and then brush it over the warm muffins. Leave in the tin for 5 minutes before placing on a wire rack to cool.

ATHOLL BROSE

INGREDIENTS

250ml whisky (I recommend
 a Jura Seven Wood)

70g oats

3 teaspoons heather honey

40ml double/whipping
 cream

On hearing that Iain MacDonald, the Lord of the Isles, was leading a rebellion against King James III, the man tasked with capturing the chieftain was the Earl of Atholl. He discovered their camp and dispatched his men to fill their well with whisky, oats and honey. When the Lord of the Isles and his troops drank from the well, they got so drunk that Atholl's men easily captured them. Personally, I think this delicious, intoxicating drink is far too good to give to your enemies! Either way, you need to start your prep at least a day before you'd like to drink it . . .

METHOD

Pour the whisky over the oats in a bowl and rest under a clean dishtowel for 24 hours.

The next day, use a muslin (or cotton dishtowel) to squeeze out the whisky into a fresh bowl. Be sure to get every last drop! You can discard the oats.

Warm up your honey for 10 seconds in the microwave – or very gently in a pan on the stove – and whisk into the Brose mix.

Add your cream and whisk again.

You can drink it now, but it's even better if you let it rest in the refrigerator for 24 hours in a sealed container. Make sure you shake it before serving. You'll find it's perfect as an after-dinner sweet treat!

GRANNY'S GRIDDLE PANCAKES

(MAKES A DOZEN)

INGREDIENTS

230g self-raising flour

60g butter

½ teaspoon cream of tartar

¼ teaspoon bicarbonate of
    soda

60g sugar

1 heaped tablespoon
    golden syrup

250ml milk

2 eggs

Granny Annag's baking was famous in the MacQueen household, and Peter's favourites were her griddle pancakes. Have your favourite dishtowel by the side of the stove and pop the pancakes in there to keep them warm while you make up your next batch.

METHOD

Rub your flour and butter together to make breadcrumbs.

Add your cream of tartar, bicarbonate of soda, sugar, golden syrup, milk and eggs. Use a knife to stir everything together.

Place heaped tablespoons of the batter on a warm griddle pan. A cast-iron skillet or frying pan will also do.

When bubbles start popping on the pancake, flip and cook for another 45 seconds.

Serve immediately with your favourite jam, honey or maple syrup.

MARMALADE TREACLE TART

INGREDIENTS

For the pastry

320g plain flour

65g icing sugar

Pinch of salt

170g cold butter, cubed

1 egg

1 orange, zested, plus
2 tablespoons of juice

1 egg yolk, to glaze

For the filling

400g golden syrup

4 tablespoons marmalade
(see page 21 to make
your own)

¼ teaspoon ground ginger

2 eggs, lightly beaten

3 tablespoons single cream

50g rolled oats

100g fresh breadcrumbs

1 lemon, zested, plus
2 teaspoons of juice

This rich, traditional Scottish tart mixes the sweetness of the golden syrup with the zestiness of the marmalade. You can make this using my homemade orange & clementine marmalade recipe on page 21.

METHOD

Preheat a baking sheet in the oven to 200°C/390°F.

To make the pasty, use a food processor to pulse the flour, icing sugar and salt. Add the butter and pulse until you make breadcrumbs. Whisk together the egg and orange juice; pour into the food processor along with the orange zest until it starts to come together.

On a worktop, shape into a flat disc, wrap in cling film and chill in the fridge for 30 minutes. Slice off a third of the pastry and return it to the fridge.

Roll out the remaining dough until it's 3mm thick, then press into a 23cm loose-bottomed tart tin. Trim around the tart tin to cut away excess pastry. Prick the base all over with a fork; chill for 20 minutes.

Line the pastry with baking paper and fill with ceramic baking beans. Blind bake on the preheated baking sheet for 20 minutes. Remove the paper and beans, then bake for 5 minutes more.

Now make the filling. Warm the syrup, marmalade and ginger in a saucepan until it begins to simmer. Cool for 5 minutes, then slowly whisk in the eggs and cream. Add the oats, breadcrumbs, lemon zest and juice. Pour the filling into the pastry case.

Reduce the oven to 180°C/360°F.

Roll out the remaining pastry to 3mm thickness and design a layer of stripes and plaits on top of the tart. Let your imagination run wild! Just leave the lengths of the lattice strips hanging over the tart tin, as the pastry may shrink while baking.

Brush the edge of the pastry case and all decorations with beaten egg yolk. Bake for 30 minutes until golden. Trim away the excess pastry with a sharp knife. Leave in the tin to settle for 15 minutes, then remove and slice.

FORAGER'S JELLY

(MAKES 6 JARS)

INGREDIENTS

1.3kg brambles, freshly picked

2 cooking apples

20 rosehips

2 limes, juiced and grated rind

750g of jam sugar for every 1 litre of juice

Brambles are wild blackberries, and if you are lucky enough to live near bramble bushes, make sure you harvest a huge batch in autumn. Brambles are too pippy to make jam – but make the best jelly in the world! You will be able to forage for rosehips at the same time; they are naturally high in pectin, which will help your jelly set. Pick these from the dog rose plant.

METHOD

Add all the fruit to a pan with just enough water to get the juices running (up to 75ml). Simmer and stir for about 25 to 30 minutes, crushing the fruit on the side of the pan with your wooden spoon.

Carefully pour the liquid through a muslin (or cotton dishtowel), tie into a bag and suspend over the pan and allow it to drip overnight. The next day, squeeze out the last drops.

On the second boil add the sugar into the pot and bring to a bubbling simmer for about 30 to 40 minutes until the temperature reaches a setting point of 105°C. A jam thermometer is very useful here!

When the jelly is ready, take off the heat and leave for 10 minutes to slightly cool down. Then fill your prepared sterilised jars. Close them tightly and leave for at least a few days to mature before eating – preferably in a chunky sandwich layered with slices of extra mature cheddar!

VEGETARIAN HAGGIS & WHISKY SAUCE

(MAKES 2 HEARTY PORTIONS)

INGREDIENTS

For the haggis

30g red lentils

1 medium onion

1 carrot, peeled

115g pinhead/steelcut oats

60g vegetarian suet

30g chopped mixed nuts

1 teaspoon salt

½ teaspoon black pepper

130ml–150ml vegetable
   stock

For the sauce

Knob of butter, melted

3–4 tablespoons whisky

1 teaspoon Dijon mustard

50ml vegetable stock

Salt and pepper to taste

100ml double/heavy cream

Trim off any large pieces of fat and cut away the windpipe is never the most appetising way to start a recipe, so I have chosen a vegetarian haggis recipe for my cookbook. It still deserves to have Rabbie Burns's 'Address to a Haggis' recited before digging in!

Address to a Haggis

Fair fa' your honest, sonsie face,
Great Chieftain o' the Puddin-race!
Aboon them a' ye tak your place,
      Painch, tripe, or thairm:
Weel are ye wordy o'a grace
      As lang's my arm.

METHOD

First make the haggis. Soak your lentils overnight and then drain.

Preheat the oven to 180°C/360°F.

Finely chop your onion and carrot, mix in with the oats, suet, lentils and nuts, then season. Add enough stock to make a moist consistency.

Butter a pudding basin, pour in your haggis and cover in foil. Bake in the oven for 25 minutes, remove the foil and bake for a further 20 minutes.

Now make your sauce. Add your whisky to the melted butter and let it simmer in a pan. Add your mustard and stock and bring it back on to simmer. Season and add your cream – let that reduce to a gravy-like thickness.

Serve your haggis with neeps and tatties – mashed turnip and potatoes – and pour over your whisky sauce. Make sure you have a dram of your favourite single malt to wash it down!

MYTHS & LEGENDS

The first story I ever remember my mother telling me was of two brothers who lived just down the road from us in the village of Calbost. These brothers were no ordinary siblings, as both were giants. One day, when out gathering their sheep, they fell out over which path home they should walk their flock. The older brother, Tormod, began to climb the path to the south and his younger brother, Torfi, took the path to the north. They continued to argue, shouting Gaelic insults at each other from across the glen. Torfi picked up a rock the size of a cow and threw it at his brother; the rock bounced off Tormod's shoulder, smashed into a thousand pieces and rolled down the hill to the shoreline. In a rage, Tormod lifted the biggest rock he could find and threw it at Torfi, who at exactly the same time threw another rock at his brother. The brothers weren't to know that the rocks they'd heaved into the air had been cursed by the *Bean-shìthe* (a fairy woman) and, as they hit, would turn them both to stone.

Now when you visit the village of Calbost, you will see two very rocky hills by the shoreline named *Mol nam Bràithrean* – The Brothers' Beach – which are made up of all the stones that rolled down to the shoreline that fateful day. My mother would take me there when the sun shone, and I would always run past those hills as fast as I could, in case the giants might see me and cast their final cursed stone.

But the most frightening of Hebridean legends are not of our giants and banshees, but of the creatures that live in the many seas and lochs around our islands. The most feared of all is the *each-uisge*, a supernatural water horse that prowls the shorelines for their prey. The *each-uisge* is a shapeshifter, disguising itself into the form that their victim would trust the most. There are many stories of it transforming into a fine horse and taking whomever rides it to the deepest depths of the loch. Or into a handsome man, who would kidnap maidens washing their clothes on the rocks of the shore. So, when you visit the islands of the Hebrides and are taking a walk along our beautiful seashores or by the lochside, be careful. All those friendly folk you meet? Well, just maybe things are not always as they first seem . . .

There was a man who lived in our village of Cromore who had two daughters, Sybil and Gormelia. The girls asked their father to build them an *àirigh* – a hut or sheiling – they could rest in when taking their cows out to the summer pastures.

Their father found a remote loch and built the *àirigh* right on the shoreline. On their first night there, after milking the cows, they lifted the porridge off the fire and put it out to cool on the ledge above the door. The sun was just setting, and they went down to the edge of the loch to bathe their feet.

Night was falling, a beautiful calm night with trout dancing on the loch, and birds singing down the slopes of *Duntatha* (the hillside by the water). Suddenly the two girls could hear loud splashing from on the other side of the loch. They realised it was an elderly woman struggling to walk. Wearily, the old woman arrived at the shoreline by the *àirigh*. When she reached the girls, they asked her, 'Where on earth are you going at this time of night? You look exhausted.'

'Oh, I am exhausted,' she replied. 'I have come from Loch Claidh, and I'm making my way to the shore in Calbost.'

The girls took pity on her and invited her in. They took the porridge off the ledge above the door and encouraged her to the table for something to eat. They looked on in surprise as the old woman devoured all their porridge. Two or three mouthfuls and it was gone. There was not a drop left for them.

'You'd better stay here with us for the night. It is far too late for you to go on now,' the girls said as they beckoned her, and she accepted their kind offer of a bed.

But when bedtime came, Sybil asked Gormelia, 'Where will she sleep tonight?'

Gormelia suggested that the old dear would be safer and cosier on the inside of the bed, next to the wall. But the old woman insisted on sleeping in the middle between the two girls.

Sometime before sunrise, Sybil awoke shivering and had the feeling something was wrong. She lifted her hand to see it was covered in blood. She looked at the old woman beside her, but it was not the old woman that lay there. The woman's body had transformed. Beside Sybil lay the *each-uisge*, sleeping, with a horrible, fearsome face, huge fangs and a beastly body covered in fur.

Sybil looked over at her sister and, much to her horror, realised that Gormelia lay dead. Sybil, fearing for her life, climbed out of the bed, quietly put on her petticoat and sneaked out the door. She made for the hills as fast as she could.

But it wasn't long before the *each-uisge* woke and realised that its next victim had disappeared. The beast set off in pursuit of Sybil.

When Sybil reached a spot behind Loch nan Eilean between Marvig and Cromore, she looked behind and saw the *each-uisge* appearing over Loch a Bhuidhe. She carried on running, but the dreadful beast was getting closer and closer. She finally neared Cromore

and could see her home, just as the sun was about to rise. Before the village wall, she turned to see the *each-uisge* gaining on her and she let out an almighty scream. Her father, who was sitting having breakfast, recognised his daughter's call and raced to fetch his bow and arrows and headed for where he thought the screams had come from. To this very day, that spot is known as *Mol Na h-Eigheachd* (Place of the Scream).

As Sybil tried to jump the wall into the safety of her village, the beast caught hold of her petticoat. In an instant, it ripped out her heart and she collapsed in a heap behind the wall, dead.

The *each-uisge* turned to see her father racing towards it, bow in hand. They chased each other as far as Loch a' Ghruagaich (Loch of the Brownie). The first arrow that hit severed the tail of the beast. The second hit its shoulder, and this was the fatal blow that killed the *each-uisge*.

As he walked home sobbing, knowing he had lost his two daughters, their father passed the *àirigh* and the loch that afterwards was named Loch Àirigh Na h-Aon Oidhche (Loch of the One Night Sheiling). No one ever went back to the *àirigh* and now only the place names of the hills and lochs around the village remind us of the fate of Sybil and Gormelia.

There is a traditional song performed by the wonderful Gaelic singer Julie Fowlis that I would like you to listen to. It is called '*Dh'èirich mi moch, b'fheàrr nach d' dh'èirich*' and you can find it on her album *alterum*. This very moving song is particularly interesting, as it is sung from the point of view of the *each-uisge*, who in all other stories is portrayed as the frightening character, but in this instance is the victim. It has been betrayed by its mortal lover, a woman who has escaped and left behind their child, which it cannot take care of. In the song – sung so hauntingly by Julie – the *each-uisge* begs her to return, but to no avail.

And so the stories of the islands are spun and spun again, speaking to us afresh in each retelling.

2
OATS

Bi gu subhach, geamnaidh,
moch-thràthach as t-Samhradh;
Bi gu curraiceach, brògach,
brochanach 's a' Gheamhradh.

In summertime be cheerful, sober and early out of bed;
In winter be hooded, well-shod and well on porridge fed.

BRIDE'S BONN

(MAKES 8 PETTICOAT TAILS)

INGREDIENTS

100g butter, slightly softened

50g golden caster sugar

100g self-raising flour

50g oats

Pinch of salt

½ teaspoon caraway seeds

Shetland Bride's Bonn was traditionally baked by the mother of the bride and broken over the bride's head as she entered the marital home after the wedding ceremony. It was intended to bless the marriage with prosperity and fertility. Guests would scramble to get a piece of the broken shortbread to put under their pillow that night, as it was supposed to give you sweet dreams.

METHOD

Preheat your oven to 150°C/300°F. You will need to butter and line a 23cm round tin.

Cream your butter and sugar together really well in a bowl with the back of a wooden spoon or a hand mixer.

Mix your flour, oats, salt and caraway seeds in a bowl and then add to the creamed butter one tablespoon at a time and mix in well.

Once it comes together, press into your prepared tin. Lightly cut 8 slices in the dough and place in the oven for 20 minutes or until golden brown.

Rest in the tin for 5 minutes, then allow to cool fully on a wire rack . . . before finding a bride to bash over the head – or simply cut into slices and serve. Sweet dreams!

CRANACHAN CHOCOLATE CUPS

(SERVES 4)

INGREDIENTS

150g white chocolate

40g oats

½ tablespoon brown sugar

100g raspberries (select
Scottish raspberries when
in season)

250ml double cream

2 tablespoons honey
(heather honey is my
favourite for this recipe)

2 tablespoons whisky
(Jura Whisky works
perfectly here)

The finest toasted Scottish oats, cream, whisky and raspberries combine to make cranachan, surely the king of Scottish desserts. For extra indulgence, I've served the cranachan in a white chocolate cup, which are easily made in silicone moulds. Perfect for a Burns Night dessert.

METHOD

Heat the white chocolate in a bowl in the microwave and stir every 30 seconds until fully melted.

Use a pastry brush to paint 2 coats of the melted chocolate into your silicone moulds, letting the first coat set before adding the second.

Heat a pan over a low heat. Toast the oats and brown sugar, stirring until the sugar has melted. Tip your oats on to greaseproof paper and leave to cool.

Mash 75g of the raspberries until smooth.

Whip the cream to stiffish peaks, then fold in the honey and whisky. Crumble the cooled oats in your hand as you add three-quarters of it to the cream. Swirl the mashed raspberries through the cream to add a ripple effect.

Remove the chocolate spheres from their moulds. Spoon in the cream and top with the remaining raspberries, oats and a drizzle of honey.

HONEY, RASPBERRY & OAT SLICE

INGREDIENTS

75g butter

60g soft brown sugar

½ teaspoon vanilla essence

25g honey

1 egg

80g self-raising flour

30g oats

60g raspberries

The long summer days make Scotland the perfect place to grow raspberries – and strawberries! I love that there is a burst of flavour in every slice, complementing the sweet honey in this simple sponge cake.

METHOD

Preheat the oven to 180°C/350°F.

Cream the butter, sugar, vanilla and honey until light and fluffy.

Next beat in the egg.

Fold in the flour and oats then finally stir in the raspberries.

Pour the mix into a lined square baking tin and bake for 20 to 25 minutes.

Once cooled, cut into slices and dust with icing sugar.

CHOCOLATE OATY CRUMBLES

(MAKES 16 BISCUITS)

INGREDIENTS

For the biscuit

125g butter

80g brown sugar

2 teaspoons golden syrup

100g oats

100g plain wholemeal flour

½ teaspoon bicarbonate
   of soda

½ teaspoon baking powder

Pinch of salt

For the topping

100g dark chocolate

30g butter

I made this a recipe for 16 biscuits (based on Hobnobs) because I know this is the number I can devour with an afternoon cuppa without blinking. Oaty, syrupy goodness smothered in dark chocolate, need I say more?

METHOD

Preheat the oven to 180°C/350°F.

Cream the butter and brown sugar until pale. Add the golden syrup and blend together.

Add the oats, flour, bicarbonate of soda, baking powder and salt.

Once it combines into a dough, wrap with cling film and pop in the fridge for 15 minutes.

Then roll the dough into tablespoon-sized balls, place on a lined baking sheet and press the top of each ball down gently, leaving plenty of room between each biscuit.

Bake for 10 to 12 minutes or until golden brown.

While the biscuits are cooling, melt the chocolate and butter together in the microwave. Stir every 20 seconds until combined.

Cover the top of each biscuit with the melted chocolate mix and spread out evenly using the back of a spoon. Leave it to set for a couple of minutes, then use a spoon to swirl the chocolate to give it a traditional Hobnob look.

CHERRY CHOCOLATE OVERNIGHT OATS

(MAKES A HEARTY BREAKFAST FOR 1)

INGREDIENTS

65g frozen cherries

1 tablespoon cocoa powder

2 teaspoon maple syrup

½ teaspoon vanilla extract

80ml almond milk

1 tablespoon natural yogurt

70g oats

1 tablespoon desiccated
  coconut

1 tablespoon dark chocolate
  chips

Handful of (defrosted)
  cherries

Why not take a day off from traditional porridge made with water and salt to enjoy this creamy, indulgent (but healthier than it seems) breakfast?

METHOD
Blend the frozen cherries, cocoa powder, maple syrup, vanilla extract and almond milk. Pour into a jar and add the natural yogurt and oats and stir well. Leave in the fridge overnight.

In the morning, top the oats with the desiccated coconut, chocolate chips and cherries.

AUTUMNAL PORRIDGE WITH APPLE & PEAR COMPOTE

(SERVES 2)

INGREDIENTS

For the compote

1 apple

1 pear

1 tablespoon butter

1 tablespoon brown sugar

½ teaspoon ground cinnamon

6 blackberries

30g dried cranberries

100ml water

For the porridge

130g oats

1 teaspoon chia seeds

1 teaspoon flaxseed

700ml coconut milk

When the mornings get darker and the cosy pyjamas are out of hibernation, this warming porridge will set you up for the day. I use coconut milk, but any plant-based milk will do. Adding chia and flaxseed will give your body a well-needed boost of fibre and antioxidants.

METHOD

First, make your compote. Core, peel and chop the apple and pear.

In a pan, melt the butter then add the sugar and cinnamon. Add the chopped fruit, blackberries and cranberries and coat in the butter.

Pour over the water, bring to the boil then reduce the heat to low and simmer, covered, for 10 to 15 minutes, or until the fruit is soft.

Meanwhile, make the porridge. Add the oats, chia seeds, flaxseed and coconut milk to a different pan and simmer for 10 minutes.

Serve in large bowls with a heaped spoon of the compote on top of the warm, creamy porridge.

MARMALADE BAKED OATS

INGREDIENTS

65g oats

75ml oat milk

½ teaspoon chia seeds

½ tablespoon maple syrup

1 wee banana

1 tablespoon marmalade
(see page 21 to make your
own)

For the topping

Handful of dried cranberries

1 teaspoon marmalade

Baked oats make it feel like you are having cake for breakfast, and this is something I fully endorse! This is one of the first bakes I tried in the airfryer and it worked perfectly – but of course the oven is fine too.

METHOD

Preheat your airfryer or the oven to 160°C/320°F.

In a blender, blitz the oats along with the oat milk, chia seeds, maple syrup, banana and marmalade. Pour into a ramekin and dot the cranberries on top. Place into the airfryer or oven for about 23 minutes. Once baked, brush with the extra marmalade while still hot, leave for a few minutes to cool and then enjoy your breakfast!

WEE OATCAKE MEN

(MAKES A DOZEN)

INGREDIENTS

200g rolled oats

50g pinhead or steel-cut
oats, plus a little extra for
dusting

½ teaspoon salt

¼ teaspoon brown sugar

75g butter

75ml boiling water

Oatcakes have been part of the Scottish diet for hundreds of years and still very popular today. You will need a traditional gingerbread man – or woman – cutter to make these. And if you are lucky enough to have a dog-shaped cutter perhaps you could make some oaty canine companions too!

METHOD

Preheat your oven to 180°C/360°F. Line a baking tray with baking paper.

Stir the rolled and pinhead oats together, then blend 100g of the oats mix you have just made to create oat flour and return to the bowl.

Add your salt and sugar.

Stir the butter into boiling water until melted, then add into the oats mix and combine until it begins to hold together in a dough.

Dust your work surface with pinhead oats and roll out the dough until it is about 5mm thick.

Use a traditional gingerbread man cookie cutter on your dough. With a palette knife lift each one onto a lined baking tray. You can continue to re-roll any scraps until all the dough is used up.

Bake for 20 minutes, switch off the oven, carefully turn the gingerbread men over and bake for 5 more minutes.

Remove from the oven and lift from the tray. Cool on a wire rack. I like to serve mine with salted butter and Hebridean Blue from Isle of Mull Cheese.

SAVOURY OATS

(MAKES A HEARTY BREAKFAST FOR 1)

INGREDIENTS

2 rashers of bacon or
    50g diced pancetta

2 spring onions

230ml water

50g oats

1 egg

Sprinkling of chopped chives

1 chilli, red or green

30g goats cheese

Salt and pepper, to season

In my quest to eat oats for every meal of the day, these savoury oats could be my new favourite weekend brunch. It takes minutes to make. You can always double the portion size – if there's two of you for breakfast!

METHOD

Dice your bacon and sizzle along with your spring onions in a pan.

Add your water to a different pan and once it is boiling, add the oats and slowly simmer for 5 minutes until thick.

To poach your egg, crack an egg into a ramekin. Then drop the egg into simmering water. Cook your egg for 3 minutes and remove with a slotted spoon.

Add your cooked oats to a bowl, stir in your bacon and spring onions.

Chop your chives, slice your chilli and goats cheese, then sprinkle on top.

Place your poached egg on top of the oaty mix and season well. Serve immediately.

SCOTS FLUMMERY

(MAKES 4 SERVINGS)

INGREDIENTS

2 tablespoons oats

450ml water

1 orange, zested and juiced

4 tablespoons sugar

150ml double cream

2 tablespoons honey

2 tablespoons whisky

According to legend, Flora MacDonald was halfway through a dish of Scots Flummery when she was arrested for her part in helping Bonnie Prince Charlie escape following his defeat at Culloden in 1746. As a last supper before going to prison, this is the perfect choice. Don't forget to soak your oats in advance!

METHOD

Soak your oats in 450ml of cold water for 48 hours, then use a muslin cloth (or clean tea-towel) to squeeze out the water into a bowl and discard the oats.

Pour the oaty water into a pan and add 6 tablespoons of orange juice and the sugar. Bring to a boil, then simmer, stirring continuously until thick (this should take about 15 minutes).

When cooled, stir in 75ml of the cream, pour into 4 glasses and chill in the fridge for 30 minutes.

Warm the honey in a saucepan over a low heat or in the microwave for 10 seconds and stir in the whisky. While cool, but still runny, add a tablespoon or so of the mix to each glass.

Whip the remaining cream and top each glass with a dollop and sprinkle with some orange zest.

MONOLITHS & MACHAIR

I could hear the phone ringing as I opened the front door. I kicked off my yellow wellies, ran into the kitchen and picked up the receiver. Before I could say hello, the voice on the other end exclaimed, 'I'm coming to visit, my trip is booked!'

I met Bethany on my first day at Glasgow University. In her signature biker jacket, this raven-haired rocker chick from Illinois seemed way too cool to hang around with an islander like me. But we became great friends. Over the years I visited her when she lived in Dallas, Chicago, Las Vegas and Nashville. And I even did a reading at her wedding to hubby Warwick. Finally, it was her turn to have a Hebridean adventure and I set about planning her trip to Lewis and Harris.

As I stood waving at the ferry arriving into Stornoway, Bethany stepped down the gangway. Not in her biker jacket, but prepared for all weathers in her waterproofs and bobble hat. We had just two days together and planned to make the most of them.

Roused by many hours watching *Outlander*, Bethany wanted her first stop to be Callanish and the standing stones that inspired the ancient stone circle of Craigh na Dun. In the first episode of the show, Claire is transported back to 1743 after placing her hands on the ancient rock. And there are very few in the world more ancient than these.

Five thousand years ago, the Isle of Lewis was the centre of sophisticated monumental building which influenced later monuments such as Stonehenge. Rows of monoliths stretch outward from this stone circle, forming a cross shape. These stones of 300-million-year-old Lewisian gneiss – some of the oldest rock on the planet – were chosen, hauled and precisely placed by our Neolithic ancestors using only stone tools, a considerable amount of strength and even greater skill.

I wonder if when Hecateaus of Abdera, a fourth-century BC Greek philosopher, wrote about the mythical people named the Hyperboreans, he was describing Hebrideans. In Greek mythology, the Hyperboreans lived in the far northern part of the known world and on their island they had *a magnificent sacred precinct of Apollo and a notable temple which is adorned with many votive offerings and is spherical in shape.* Perhaps I'm being fanciful, but I like the idea of us Hebrideans being thought of as mythical people!

Myths and legends surround the stones. Stories range from them being used as a place of ritual, a centre of worship, an astronomical observatory or even that they were once giants who were turned to stone by St Kieran after they did not convert to Christianity.

As we stand between them watching the sun rise over the hills that form the shape of a reclining woman named *Cailleach na Mòinteach* – 'old woman of the moors' – Bethany closes her eyes and presses her hand onto one of the stones. She might not have been transported back in time, but she is definitely moved by the mysteries that surround these ancient monoliths.

We cross the narrow bridge over to the island of Great Bernera. Driving through the rocky landscape to the furthest corner of the island, where we see the hidden beach at Bosta sparkle in the sunlight. We grab our picnic of island treats bought from Stag Bakery and Charlie Barley's Butcher as well as a couple of slices of my Aunt Bellag's homemade duff and walk towards the Atlantic waters.

The beach overlooks the outer fringes of Loch Roag towards Little Berneray, Flodday, Campay and Bearsay and is hugged by the colourful machair. *Machair* is a Gaelic word meaning fertile low-lying grassy plain. It refers to a unique habitat that is one of the rarest in Europe; it only occurs on the exposed west-facing shores of Scotland and Ireland.

Here, traditional Hebridean crofting practices and sand – largely made up of crushed shells blown ashore by Atlantic gales – have led to the development of a mosaic of wildflowers and fertile grasslands home to much of the island's bird and insect life.

For these few weeks every year, a carpet of ox-eye daisies, red clover, harebell, buttercups and Hebridean spotted orchids bring a welcome, delicate burst of colour to the islands.

Undeterred by the foreboding dark clouds, we head south to the Isle of Harris early the next morning. We need to be at Leverburgh Harbour at 8 a.m. for a trip to the island archipelago of St Kilda. St Kilda is one of the few UNESCO World Heritage Sites to hold dual status for its natural and cultural qualities. Breathtakingly remote and isolated, it is a truly extraordinary place.

The first written record of St Kilda dates from 1202 when an Icelandic cleric wrote of taking shelter on 'the islands that are called Hirtir'. Nearly a thousand years later, St Kilda is seen as a place of epic adventure – a visit to which is genuinely a once-in-a-lifetime experience.

But for thousands of years, these islands were inhabited. St Kilda's distance from the rest of the Outer Hebrides (lying 41 miles off the west coast of Benbecula) allowed for the development of a unique style of self-sufficient island life for its population, at times numbering as many as 180. Freshwater springs made

life on the main island of Hirta possible, and for centuries the islanders survived by eating the meat and eggs of seabirds – hunted and harvested by men on ropes descending some of Europe's highest cliffs – fish caught near the islands, and such barley, oats and potatoes as they could grow and store to last the winter. A stone bothy – known as a *cleit* – uniquely found on the islands of St Kilda was used to store their food.

The islanders kept Soay sheep on Hirta and on the smaller islands of Soay and Borerary, a breed well suited to the harsh and precipitous island conditions, and which produced a distinctive soft wool.

Even so, life on Hirta was a constant challenge. Not only were these volcanic islands struck by frequent severe Atlantic storms, the eighteenth century brought cholera and smallpox that devastated the population. Over the next two hundred years, St Kilda's population was ravaged by infant mortality, famine and gradual depopulation.

After the harsh winter of 1929–30, the St Kilda community was in a precarious state. Only thirty-six islanders remained. The decision to evacuate the island archipelago was taken because life there was becoming untenable. The islanders wrote to the government to 'pray and petition' to help them leave the island and to find homes and occupation on the mainland.

And so, the last residents of St Kilda left the island on the 29th of August 1930. Thirty-six men, women and children watched as the HMS *Harebell* arrived at the island's harbour to take them away. As they closed their doors for the final time, each family said a prayer, leaving a bible and a handful of oats behind in their homes.

Now, two and a half hours after leaving Leverburgh, Bethany and I see the dramatic sea cliffs appear in front of us, and my thoughts go to that day nearly one hundred years ago and how difficult it would have been for the community to take the heart-wrenching decision to leave. But also how fortunate we are to be able to visit and get even just a small insight into what life would have been like for them.

The islands are home to Europe's largest colony of seabirds and, as we land, the sky is filled with what is surely thousands of gannets. We climb off the boat just as those dark clouds break and the rain pours down on us. We spend our day with our waterproofs on, hiking up the hills, walking through the village and trying to get that perfect photo of a puffin – there's plenty to choose from, after all, as there are 140,000 pairs of puffins nesting on the island! It is a place of extraordinary, dramatic and stunning beauty. And, unlike those who left their homes on that day in 1930, I hope I get the chance to return.

Two weeks later, a postcard drops through the letterbox. It has a picture of Dolly Parton on the front with the saying: *The way I see it, if you want the rainbow, you gotta put up with the rain.* On the back were the simple words:

Best holiday ever, love Bethany x

3
BAKES &
LOAVES

Cho sona ri luch ann an lof

As happy as a mouse in a loaf.

CARROT & CARDAMOM CAKE

INGREDIENTS

For the cake

100g soft brown sugar

1 egg

70 ml vegetable oil

150g carrot, grated

50g raisins

20g pistachios, unsalted and shelled

5 cardamom pods

90g self-raising flour

¼ teaspoon bicarbonate of soda

Pinch of grated nutmeg

For the icing

20g butter

60g full-fat cream cheese

40g icing sugar

½ a lime, zested and juiced

Small handful of pistachios, coarsely chopped

A traditional carrot cake is probably my favourite bake of all. The cardamom enhances the spices with a lemon and mint hit. Always use the seeds from cardamom pods if you can, rather than pre-ground.

METHOD

Preheat your oven to 150°C/300°F.

Cream your brown sugar and egg together before slowly whisking in the vegetable oil.

Add your grated carrot along with the raisins. Coarsely chop your shelled pistachios and stir in.

Remove the seeds from the cardamom pods and grind in a pestle and mortar. Add along with the flour, bicarbonate of soda and some freshly grated nutmeg.

Pour into a 1lb loaf tin and place in the oven for 35 to 40 minutes until a skewer comes out clean. Rest in the tin for 5 minutes before placing on a wire rack.

For the icing, cream the butter and then whip in the cream cheese. Combine the icing sugar (make sure you sieve it in) and the zest and juice of half a lime.

Leave your icing mix in the fridge to set for 30 minutes before smothering liberally over the cake and then sprinkle some more pistachios on top.

LEMON & POPPY SEED ROULADE

INGREDIENTS

For the cake

3 eggs

150g sugar

1 lemon, zested and juiced
(you will need
3 tablespoons of juice)

100g plain flour

1 teaspoon baking powder

¼ teaspoon salt

Handful of icing sugar to help
roll the cake

For the filling

250ml double cream

100g white chocolate, melted

150g full-fat cream cheese

20g poppy seeds

½ a lemon, zested and juiced
(you will need
1 tablespoon of juice)

60g lemon curd (homemade
is best, if you have it!)

My niece Christina worked at the famous Stag Bakery on the Isle of Lewis
for many years, and her husband Ted still does. It takes a little effort to get
right, but her twist on a classic lemon and poppy seed cake is inspired –
and delicious.

METHOD

Preheat your oven to 180°C/350°F.

Beat the eggs at high speed for 2 minutes until frothy and airy, then beat in
the sugar, lemon juice and zest.

Sieve the flour, baking powder and salt into a bowl and then stir into the
egg mixture until blended.

Line and butter a 36cm x 25cm Swiss roll tin and pour in the batter. Make
sure it goes all the way to the corners and give the tin a tap to bring up any
air bubbles.

Bake in the oven for 9 to 11 minutes.

Set a clean kitchen towel out on your work surface and sprinkle liberally
with icing sugar. As soon as the cake comes out of the oven, turn it onto the
kitchen towel and slowly remove the greaseproof paper.

Place another clean, dampened kitchen towel on top and carefully roll to
create the roulade effect – it's like a Swiss roll. Once rolled, leave the cake
to rest in the towels.

While the cake is cooling, add your double cream to a bowl and whisk
until soft peaks have formed.

In another bowl, stir together melted white chocolate, cream cheese, poppy
seeds, lemon juice and zest. Fold into the double cream and leave to rest in
the fridge for 15 minutes.

Once cooled, unroll the roulade. Spread it with a thin layer of lemon curd
and then spoon your poppy seed cream mixture on top. Spread evenly,
then carefully roll tightly back up.

Wrap the roll in cling film and place in the fridge for an hour. Remove, dust
with icing sugar, garnish with lemon zest and serve.

GINGER LOAF

And here is Peter's favourite of my bakes. I make it extra gingery (is that even a word?!) by adding ginger paste. It can be served plain, but I love an orange butter icing smothered on top.

INGREDIENTS

For the loaf

90g soft brown sugar

90g butter

90g golden syrup

2 teaspoons ginger paste

100ml milk

1 egg

125g plain flour

1 teaspoon ground ginger

½ teaspoon mixed spice

¾ teaspoon bicarbonate of
soda

For the icing

75g butter

150g icing sugar

1 orange, zested

1 tablespoon of orange juice

METHOD

Preheat your oven to 180°C/350°F.

Into a saucepan add your brown sugar, butter, golden syrup and ginger paste. Stir over a low heat until the butter has melted and the ingredients have combined. Now let that cool for 5 minutes.

Stir in your milk and whisk in an egg.

In a separate bowl sieve in your flour, ground ginger, mixed spice and bicarbonate of soda. Make a well in the middle and pour in your mixture and combine. Place in a greased loaf tin.

Before putting the tin in the oven, bang it on your work surface to knock out any air bubbles. Place in the oven for 32 to 34 minutes. Leave to cool in the tin for 5 minutes before turning out onto a wire rack.

To make the icing, cream your butter until soft before slowly sieving in your icing sugar. Grate your orange and add the zest along with a tablespoon of the juice. Combine together before chilling in the fridge for 15 minutes and then covering the loaf.

SPICED TEA CAKE

INGREDIENTS

For the cake

300ml black tea, made using a teabag of your choice

250g mixed dried fruit

280g self-raising flour

200g soft brown sugar

1 teaspoon cinnamon

1 teaspoon mixed spice

½ teaspoon nutmeg, freshly grated

1 tablespoon black treacle

2 eggs

For the icing

220g butter, softened

340g icing sugar

2 teaspoons vanilla extract

2 teaspoons mixed spice

220g full-fat cream cheese, at room temperature

For the topping

Small handful of pistachios, coarsely chopped

When you make your morning cup of tea, start the prep for this cake and it will be ready for your afternoon treat. Choose Earl Grey or Chai tea to give this cake an extra burst of flavour.

METHOD

Preheat your oven to 180°C/350°F.

Cover a teabag with 300ml of boiling water and allow to completely cool as it infuses. Take the teabag out, then pour this over your dried fruit and leave to soak for 4 hours.

Add the flour, sugar, cinnamon, mixed spice and freshly grated nutmeg to a bowl. Pour in the soaked fruit (along with any of the leftover liquid) and stir together.

Add the black treacle and eggs and combine.

Grease and line two 20cm sandwich tins, add an even amount of the mixture to each and place in the oven for 25 to 30 minutes or until a skewer comes out clean.

Leave to cool in the tins for 5 minutes before turning out onto a wire rack.

Now make the icing. Put the softened butter in a bowl and mix until smooth. Add the icing sugar, vanilla extract and mixed spice. Beat on a medium speed for 3 minutes until light and fluffy.

Add chunks of cream cheese to the mixing bowl and beat until everything is combined. You might need to place in the fridge for 15 minutes to set. Then spread liberally on one of the cakes, place the second on top and spread the rest of the mixture on top of that. For some added crunch and colour, scatter chopped pistachios to decorate.

RABARBRAKAKE

INGREDIENTS

75g butter

75g sugar

1 egg

1 egg yolk

5 cardamom pods

100g plain flour

¾ teaspoon baking powder

¾ teaspoon almond extract

60ml milk

125g rhubarb

Raspberries, a handful

Flaked almonds, a handful

I don't know why, but the word for rhubarb in Gaelic – *rùbrab* – is my favourite! In Norwegian, it's *rabarbra*. So here's my Norwegian rhubarb cake.

METHOD

Preheat the oven 180°C/350°F. Grease and line a 15cm round tin.

Cream your butter and sugar together until pale, then whisk in your egg and egg yolk.

Remove the seeds from the cardamom pods and grind in a pestle and mortar. Add along with the flour, baking powder, almond extract and milk and combine.

Chop your rhubarb into smallish chunks and stir half of it into your batter.

Pour your batter into your prepared tin. Then press the remaining rhubarb on top along with a handful of raspberries. Sprinkle on your flaked almonds and place in the oven for 40 minutes or until a skewer comes out clean.

Serve warm with a dollop of crème fraîche.

PARSNIP CAKE

INGREDIENTS

For the loaf

100g soft brown sugar

1 egg

70ml vegetable oil

100g parsnip, grated

50g apple, grated

1 clementine, zested and
    juiced

90g self-raising flour

¼ teaspoon bicarbonate of
    soda

½ teaspoon cinnamon

¼ teaspoon nutmeg, grated

For the glaze

125g icing sugar

15ml warm water

I love parsnips roasted with a honey glaze as a side dish for Sunday dinner, but if you have a couple left over, the sweet and nutty taste of parsnip is perfect for baking.

METHOD

Preheat your oven to 150°C/300°F.

Cream your brown sugar and egg together before slowly whisking in the vegetable oil.

Grate your parsnip and apple and add to the bowl along with the juice and zest of a clementine.

Sieve in your flour, bicarbonate of soda, cinnamon and fresh grated nutmeg and combine.

Place in a lined and greased 1lb loaf tin and place in the oven for 35 minutes or until a skewer comes out clean. Leave to cool in the tin for 5 minutes before turning out onto a wire rack.

To make the glaze, sift the icing sugar into a bowl and gradually add the warm water until the icing becomes thick enough to coat the back of a spoon. Take a spoonful and pattern the top of the fully cooled cake.

BRA BRAW BUNS

(MAKES 10 TO 12)

INGREDIENTS

For the dough

500g strong white flour

2½ teaspoons dried yeast

70g sugar

Pinch of salt

½ teaspoon ground
cardamom

75g butter

250ml lukewarm milk

For the filling

200g lingonberry jam
(if you can't get
lingonberry, replace
with your favourite jam)

100g white chocolate chips

For the topping

Egg, beaten with a little milk

Pearl sugar (also known as
nib sugar)

My sister-in-law Seonag is half Swedish, half Hebridean. *Bra* is the Swedish for good, with *braw* being the Scots version of the same word. Seonag's twist on the traditional Swedish cinnamon bun will definitely leave you exclaiming how 'good-good' they are!

METHOD

Combine the flour, yeast, sugar, salt and cardamom in a bowl. Melt the butter and add lukewarm milk to the dry ingredients a little at a time until you get a nice soft dough. Knead for 10 minutes then leave for an hour or until the dough doubles in size.

After the dough has doubled in size, knock it back – use the heels of your hands or fist until it is smooth and all the air is knocked out. Now roll it out to roughly a 25cm x 35cm rectangle, spread the jam evenly over the dough then sprinkle with the chocolate chips. Roll it up like a Swiss roll and pinch to secure it. Cut into about 10 to 12 slices and place in a greased brownie-size tray for a tear and share type bread.

Leave to rise again for around 45 minutes then brush with egg wash and sprinkle with pearl sugar and bake at 190°C/375°F for 20 to 25 minutes.

Leave to cool, then tear and share!

RHUBARB & CUSTARD VICTORIA SPONGE

INGREDIENTS

For the sponge

4 eggs

225g sugar

225g self-raising flour

2 teaspoons baking powder

225g butter

For the buttercream

75g butter, softened

150g icing sugar

½ teaspoon vanilla extract

2 tablespoons custard powder

2 tablespoons milk

For the finish

200g rhubarb jam

Icing sugar, to dust

Those who enjoy the classic flavour combination of rhubarb and custard will love this twist on the iconic Victoria Sponge.

METHOD

Preheat the oven to 180°C/350°F.

This recipe uses the all-in-one method. Into a bowl add your eggs, sugar, flour, baking powder and butter. Combine with a hand mixer, but don't over mix.

Grease and line two 20cm sandwich tins. Divide the mixture evenly between the tins.

Bake the cakes for 20 to 25 minutes. The cakes are done when they're golden-brown and a skewer comes out clean. Set aside to cool in their tins for 5 minutes before turning out onto a wire rack.

To make the custard buttercream, beat all the ingredients together until smooth, light and fluffy, using a hand mixer.

To assemble, put one sponge upside down on a serving plate and spread the jam over the top, then pipe on the buttercream. Place the other sponge on top. Dust with icing sugar to serve.

MORVEN'S APPLE DAPPY LOAF

INGREDIENTS

90g butter

90g sugar

90g self-raising flour

2 eggs

1 medium cooking apple, peeled

1 lemon, zested

Cinnamon powder, to serve

Peter's mum Morven told me this was his favourite cake growing up and now it's one of mine. Beautiful light sponge with soft apple chunks – as we say in Gaelic, *blasta!*

METHOD

Preheat the oven to 180°C/350°F.

Into a bowl add the butter, sugar, flour and eggs and combine together with a hand mixer.

Peel and chop your apple into wee chunks. Add to the batter along with the zest of a lemon.

Place in a loaf tin and bake for 30 minutes until a skewer comes out clean.

Leave it to cool in the tin for 5 minutes before turning it out onto a wire rack to cool fully. Dust with cinnamon powder and serve.

MADAINN MHATH BUNS

(MAKES A DOZEN)

INGREDIENTS

225ml milk

25g butter

½ a lemon, grated rind

250g strong white bread
   flour

250g plain (all-purpose) flour

1 teaspoon salt

50g sugar

7g fast action dried yeast

1 large egg, whisked

1 jar lemon curd, ideally
   homemade

For the icing

250g icing sugar

1 lemon, zested and juiced

I met Magz, known as @Hebridean, on TikTok and we bonded over
a shared passion for our island, language, culture, food and the vital
importance of good wellington boots! Magz runs the Mill View Guesthouse
on the Isle of Lewis, and these Madainn Mhath Buns (which is the Gaelic for
'good morning') are a favourite breakfast treat among her guests. And now
that I've tasted these iced lemon curd delights, I can see why!

METHOD

Pour the milk into a pan with the butter and lemon rind. Warm over a gentle
heat until the butter begins to melt.

Sift the flours into the bowl of a stand mixer with dough hook attached.
Add the salt, sugar and yeast (keeping the yeast on the opposite side of the
bowl to the salt).

Pour in the warm, lemony milk, and add the whisked egg. Set the mixer on a
slow speed for 7 to 8 minutes.

Pop the dough into a large, oiled bowl, cover loosely with oiled cling film
and allow it to prove and double in size for a couple of hours. When the
dough has risen, knock it back – use the heels of your hands or fist until it is
smooth and all the air is knocked out – then divide into 12 pieces.

Flatten each of the individual pieces then roll up into fingers roughly 20cm
long. Place the fingers onto an oiled Swiss roll tin, cover again with oiled
cling film, and prove in a warm spot to once again double in size.

Meanwhile, preheat your oven to 200°C/390°F. For billowy soft rolls,
place a roasting tin with hot water in the bottom of your hot oven to create
steam while your rolls bake.

Once the rolls have proved, bake them for 10 to 15 minutes, until well risen
and a light golden brown colour.

Allow the rolls to cool. Slice in half and add a big dollop of lemon curd in
each.

To make the lemon glacé icing, simply sift the sugar into a bowl then stir in
the lemon zest and enough lemon juice to make a thick, pourable glaze.
Use this to ice each bun thickly.

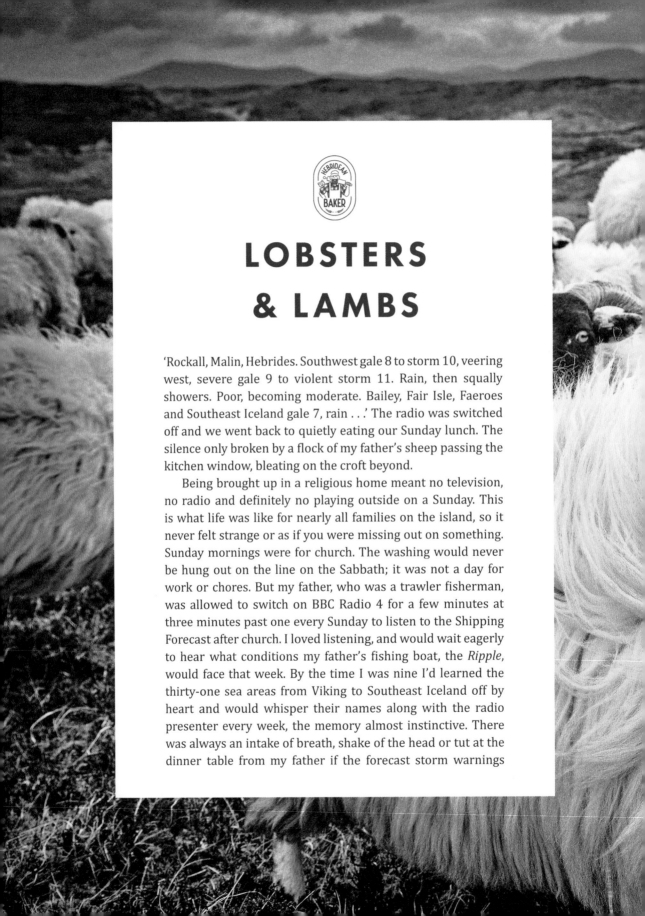

LOBSTERS & LAMBS

'Rockall, Malin, Hebrides. Southwest gale 8 to storm 10, veering west, severe gale 9 to violent storm 11. Rain, then squally showers. Poor, becoming moderate. Bailey, Fair Isle, Faeroes and Southeast Iceland gale 7, rain . . .' The radio was switched off and we went back to quietly eating our Sunday lunch. The silence only broken by a flock of my father's sheep passing the kitchen window, bleating on the croft beyond.

Being brought up in a religious home meant no television, no radio and definitely no playing outside on a Sunday. This is what life was like for nearly all families on the island, so it never felt strange or as if you were missing out on something. Sunday mornings were for church. The washing would never be hung out on the line on the Sabbath; it was not a day for work or chores. But my father, who was a trawler fisherman, was allowed to switch on BBC Radio 4 for a few minutes at three minutes past one every Sunday to listen to the Shipping Forecast after church. I loved listening, and would wait eagerly to hear what conditions my father's fishing boat, the *Ripple*, would face that week. By the time I was nine I'd learned the thirty-one sea areas from Viking to Southeast Iceland off by heart and would whisper their names along with the radio presenter every week, the memory almost instinctive. There was always an intake of breath, shake of the head or tut at the dinner table from my father if the forecast storm warnings

were high, but even so, for five days a week he would head out in the north Atlantic with his crew to fish for prawns. But even after he got home on a Friday, he would take his wee rowing boat out to check his creels for lobsters and crabs. Fishing and the seas around the island of Lewis were his life, a life that meant my mam had plenty of fresh fish to put on the table for dinner in the evenings.

My father loved telling a story – I definitely inherited that from him – the question was always just how much truth was in the story! I would often catch my mother rolling her eyes as he began the telling of one of his tall tales. And my favourite was about the day he met the Queen . . .

It was a sunny day in August 1988 and I had just turned fourteen. I'd got a new bike for my birthday and was cycling through my home village of Cromore. This wee hamlet of about thirty croft houses scattered over hills and by the shoreline sits on the southeast coast of the island. The road ended at our village and it was rare for the peace and tranquillity to be broken. So, when I saw a huge boat on the horizon, I headed down to the pier

to find out what was going on. In the distance, I could see a rowing boat coming towards the village. Are we being attacked? was my first thought (I was quite dramatic, even as a kid), but no, the men on the boat told me they were from the Royal Yacht *Britannia*. Queen Elizabeth II was sailing to her Scottish home at Balmoral and they had broken down just outside our village. These men were the crew, all being volunteers from the general service of the Royal Navy. I took them for a walk around Cromore and proudly showed them our bright red phone box (not every village had one, so I thought it would impress them). They headed back to their boat, I waved them away and went to tell everyone my story. This summer's day encounter felt like the most momentous thing that had ever happened to me.

Meanwhile, there was an even bigger story brewing. Over the past thirty years, this tale has been told so many times that there must be at least ten different versions. But here is my favourite.

My father was rowing home after a bountiful day checking his creels. Suddenly he felt a crash and turned around to find he'd

bumped into the Royal Yacht *Britannia*. Leaning over the side of the yacht was the Queen and her sister Princess Margaret, who was – naturally enough – smoking a cigarette. The Queen asked where my father had been.

'Out checking my creels, I had a good day!' he replied. 'Do you have anything in for dinner tonight?'

Then, according to my father, the Queen replied, 'No.'

'Would you like some shellfish?' he asked.

'Oh yes,' she replied.

So, my father filled a creel with lobsters and crabs and threw a rope up to Princess Margaret, who pulled the creel up and expertly emptied it on the deck of the yacht.

The Queen then exclaimed, 'I don't carry money, how can I pay you?'

My father waved the question away, telling her they were a gift. Just before Princess Margaret passed the creel back to my father, she placed a packet of her cigarettes into it, then waved to my father as he rowed back to land.

My father, who liked a dram or two of whisky, spent the next few hours visiting all the houses in the village telling his story. So, by the time he got home to tell us, he was a bit worse for wear and, as with most of the stories he told, we weren't exactly sure how much of it was true. But as he showed us the packet of cigarettes that Princess Margaret had given him, we did begin to wonder – where would he have got them from? The nearest shop was thirty miles away.

Weeks went by and the story had already passed into folklore along with the Loch Ness Monster and Robert the Bruce and his wee spider. So, when the man who lived across the loch appeared at the door, we had nearly forgotten of my father's adventure. This man had the same name as my father, Dòmhnall Iain MacLeòid, and after he'd caught his breath, exclaimed in Gaelic to my father, 'I think this letter is for you!' We all looked at the envelope with the royal stamp ERII in the bottom left-hand corner. As my father opened it, we could see the notepaper was from the H.M. Yacht *Britannia* . . . and so he read:

Dear Mr MacLeod,

I am commanded by the Queen to write and thank you for your generous gift of lobsters. Her Majesty was delighted to receive them and enjoyed the delicious taste of fresh lobster.

Unfortunately, after you left us, our engine broke down, so we didn't catch as many mackerel and pollack as we had hoped.

I am to thank you once again and to say how the Queen appreciated your kindness.

Yours sincerely,

Kathyrn Dupdale,

Lady in Waiting

As the whole family and our neighbour stood around speechless, my father folded up the letter and began another story, this time about some lost sheep.

We'll never know how much of the story was actually true, but one thing is for sure, I can always say that my father gave the Queen crabs!

Life went back to normal after that eventful day and even if much has changed on the island in the intervening decades – on Sundays, though still sombre, you can now fly to the town of Stornoway from the mainland, fill your tank up with petrol and even enjoy a hearty meal at a local hotel – much in our family has not. My oldest brother Dòmhnall, named after my father, was a fisherman for over twenty-five years, my brothers Murdo and Colin still rear sheep and between them will sell over four hundred lambs a year. Fishing and crofting have been the mainstay of our family for centuries. I hope it stays that way for a few more centuries to come.

4
FROM THE LAND TO THE SEA

Fàilte gu fearann air balaich an iasgaich
'G iomradh 's a' tarraing 's a' gearradh a' bhiathaidh
Coma leam leabaidh no cadal no biadh
Gu faigh mi mo lìon an òrdugh.

Welcome ashore the fisher lads
Rowing and hauling and cutting the bait
I don't care for bed, sleep or food
Until I get my net in order.

PEA & HAM SOUP

INGREDIENTS

750g smoked ham hock

1 onion

1 leek

3 celery sticks

3 peeled potatoes,
   roughly 400g

Knob of butter

1 teaspoon black pepper

800g frozen peas

1 tablespoon crème fraîche

There was a classic television advert for stock cubes in the 1980s, where Hughie tells his pal that it's chicken soup for dinner as he and his wife had enjoyed roast chicken the night before. Unbeknownst to him, his wife had in fact used Knorr ham stock cubes.

When he is asked the next day how the soup was, he exclaimed, 'The remarkable thing was it wisnae chicken, it was Pea and Ham.' To which his pal uttered the now immortal words: 'Pea and ham, fae a chicken? Now that's clever!'

It doesn't matter who I make this soup for, the moment I serve it . . . well, someone at the table will say that line! But no stock cubes are harmed in my recipe! I use the ham hock, which is the bottom half of the pork leg.

METHOD

Place the ham hock in a deep pan with 1.25 litres of water and simmer for 2 hours.

Take off the heat and remove the ham from the stock, reserving the ham stock to make the soup.

Chop the onion, leek, celery and potatoes, then sauté in butter until soft.

To the ham stock, add your sautéed vegetables, pepper (no salt, the stock will be salty enough from the hock) and 750g of your peas. Pull the ham off the bone, cut into wee pieces, add half to the soup and simmer for 15 minutes.

Use a hand-held blender to purée everything. Finally stir in the leftover peas and the crème fraîche.

Serve the soup topped with shredded ham.

BURNS NIGHT CULLEN SKINK

INGREDIENTS

250g smoked haddock

150ml cold water

1 bay leaf

1 onion

1 leek

1 tablespoon butter

400g potatoes

250ml milk

Salt and pepper to season
(or 1 teaspoon of Mara
Seaweed Shony Flakes)

2 spring onions, chopped,
to serve

This fish soup originates from the town of Cullen in Moray, on the northeast coast of Scotland. And though there are many variations, this is my favourite to serve on Burns Night before the traditional Toast to the Haggis.

METHOD

Place the haddock in a pan on a medium heat and cover with about 150ml cold water and add the bay leaf. By the time it comes to the boil, the fish should be just cooked. Set the fish aside, but keep the stock.

Sauté the chopped onion and leek in butter for 5 minutes until they have softened.

Chop the potato into wee squares, add them to the sautéed onion and leek, then pour in the stock from the haddock and simmer until the potato is tender.

Remove the skin and any bones from the haddock and break into chunky flakes.

Lift out half the potatoes, onions and leeks, and set aside. Add the milk, and half the haddock to the pan and mash roughly. I season with seaweed flakes, but sea salt and pepper will be just as delicious too.

Serve a ladle of the soup and top with a generous spoonful of the chunky potato, leek and haddock mixture in each bowl. Finally, scatter a sprinkling of spring onions.

GIN GRAVADLAX WITH BEETROOT & APPLE SALAD

INGREDIENTS

For the Gravadlax

2 x 200g salmon fillets (pinboned, with the skin left on)

60g sea salt

1 tablespoon peppercorns

60g sugar

35ml gin

1 lemon, zested (save the juice for the salad)

Bunch of fresh dill

For the salad

250g jar of pickled beetroot

½ eating apple, peeled; a Braeburn apple will work well

3 tablespoons mayonnaise

3 tablespoons crème fraîche

Squeeze of lemon juice

Salt and pepper, to season

I'm channelling my inner Scandinavian by curing my salmon to create a delicious Gravadlax accompanied by a colourful Rödbetsallad for this recipe. Start the curing process the day before you plan to go full Viking.

METHOD

To make the cure, blitz the salt, peppercorns, sugar, gin, lemon zest and a large handful of fresh dill together in a food processor. Set some dill aside for the next stage, too.

Next, lay your salmon fillets skin side down on a sheet of cling film and spread the cure all over. Wrap the cling film tightly around the salmon. Place on a baking tray and put another baking tray on top, weigh it down nicely with some tins from the cupboard. Put it in the fridge for 24 hours.

Next day, place a layer of finely chopped dill on a chopping board. Unwrap the salmon, carefully rinse the cure off under the cold tap, pat dry and roll the salmon in the dill. Carve the salmon into thin slices.

For the salad, simply chop the beetroot and peeled apple into 1.5cm cubes. Put in a bowl with the mayonnaise, crème fraîche, a squeeze of lemon juice and salt and pepper. Served along with the Gravadlax, this is a perfect weekend lunch.

COURGETTE SCONES

(MAKES 4)

INGREDIENTS

225g self-raising flour

1 teaspoon baking powder

55g butter, at room
    temperature

170g courgette (roughly
    one large courgette)

1 tablespoon salt

60g mature Cheddar, grated

½ teaspoon mustard powder

7 tablespoons milk

1 egg, to glaze the scones

Peter grew lots of courgettes in the garden last season and this was one of our favourite recipes to use up our bountiful crop. For those of you who are Marmite lovers, add a teaspoon to the mix to give it an even more distinctive flavour.

METHOD

Preheat the oven to 220°C/430°F.

Sift the flour and baking powder into a bowl, then add the soft butter and rub it in with your fingertips until the mixture resembles breadcrumbs.

Grate the courgettes (no need to peel them), and place in a bowl then mix in the salt. Place in muslin (or a clean tea towel) and squeeze out as much liquid as you can. Add the courgettes into the flour and butter mix along with the grated cheese and mustard powder and use your hands to stir well.

Add the milk. I use a knife to stir and make into a dough.

On a lightly floured work surface roll out the dough to about 2.5cm deep, but be careful not to work too much with the dough. Cut into 4 hearty-sized scones and brush with egg.

Place on a greased baking tray and bake for 18 to 20 minutes until the scones are well risen and golden brown. Make sure you have lots of salted butter to hand when serving!

TATTIE SCONES

(MAKES ABOUT 8)

INGREDIENTS

350g potatoes

2 eggs

50g butter, plus extra for
    griddling

1 teaspoon baking powder

1 teaspoon salt

250g plain flour

You can't have a proper full Scottish breakfast without potato scones, and once you made them at home, you won't go back to shop bought!

METHOD

Boil your potatoes in salted water, drain and let them dry out completely in the pan.

Mash the potatoes and add the eggs, butter, baking powder, salt and flour. Use your hands to blend it all together and flatten out to about a 2cm thickness.

Cut the dough into a batch of chunky scones; you can choose to make them squares or triangles.

Griddle in butter for 4 to 5 minutes each side. A griddle pan is perfect for this, but if you don't have one a flat or cast-iron frying pan does the trick.

Serve in a crusty roll with bacon (or Lorne sausage), poached egg, black pudding and lots of tomato ketchup. Vegetarian alternatives are pretty tasty too!

HEBRIDEAN PASTY

(MAKES 2 HEARTY PASTIES)

INGREDIENTS

For the pastry

250g strong bread flour

15g butter

60g vegetable shortening
or suet

½ teaspoon salt

90ml cold water

1 egg, beaten with a pinch
salt, for glazing

For the filling

85g onions

100g swede

175g potatoes

Salt and freshly ground black
pepper

175g hot smoked salmon

Knob of butter

Our Celtic cousins in Cornwall inspired me to recreate their iconic Cornish Pasty with a twist. Instead of the traditional beef, I use Scottish hot smoked salmon. These pasties are ideal for a picnic, as they can be enjoyed hot or cold.

METHOD

You can buy ready-made shortcrust pastry, but here's how you make it at home.

Add the flour, butter, shortening or suet, salt and water into a bowl and with a spoon combine the ingredients.

Begin to use your hands – you will be left with quite a dry dough. Knead the dough vigorously for about 5 minutes until it becomes smooth. Wrap in cling film and allow to rest in the fridge for an hour.

Peel and chop your onion, swede and potato into wee 1cm squares, mix and season well in a bowl.

Preheat the oven to 170°C/340°F.

Divide the pastry dough in half and roll out each into a 25cm round. Spoon half of the vegetable mix onto one half of each round and lay half of the salmon on top, then add a knob of butter on top.

Brush the pastry all the way round the edge with the beaten egg. Fold the pastry over, push with your fingers to seal. A traditional pasty is crimped around the edge 20 times by making small twists along the sealed edge.

Put the pasties onto a lined baking tray and brush the top with the egg. Bake for 40 minutes or until the pasties are golden brown.

LAMB & ALE SHEPHERD'S PIE

INGREDIENTS

For the lamb

1kg shoulder of lamb

Salt and pepper, to season

1 tablespoon olive oil

2 onions

1 garlic clove

2 carrots

2 celery sticks

Handful of fresh rosemary

500ml bottle of dark ale, your local favourite

150ml beef stock, made from a stock cube is fine

For the topping

1kg potatoes

30g butter

50ml milk

Sea salt and pepper, to season

This is slow cooking Hebridean style! Prepare the meat the day before to get the best out of the dish. This would make a perfect, wholesome winter Sunday lunch with friends. You can choose your local favourite ale to flavour the pie. Mine is Poacher from the Loomshed Brewery on the Isle of Harris.

METHOD

Preheat the oven to 120°C/250°F.

Season the lamb shoulder with salt and pepper. Heat a large casserole dish over a medium heat, add the olive oil and the lamb and fry quickly on each side until browned.

Meanwhile, finely slice the onions, chop the garlic and roughly chop the carrots and celery. Remove the lamb and set aside. Add the onions, garlic, carrots and celery to the pan and cook on a low heat for 5 minutes.

Return the lamb to the casserole, then add the chopped rosemary, ale and beef stock. Put the lid on, then transfer to the oven and cook for 5 hours.

Once cooked, tear the meat apart using a fork, mix back into the casserole, leave to cool then place in the fridge overnight.

The next day, preheat the oven to 180°C/350°F.

Now, cut the potatoes into chunks. (I don't peel my potatoes, but you can!) Bring a pan of salted water to the boil, add the potatoes and cook until fork tender. Drain well, leave to steam for a couple of minutes and then mash until smooth. Add the butter and milk and mash again, then season.

Place the lamb casserole into a big oven-proof dish and spoon over the mashed potatoes, pressing them down gently. Return to the oven and cook for another 25 minutes until hot, golden and bubbling. Serve with steamed green beans.

LOBSTER MAC(LEOD) 'N' CHEESE

INGREDIENTS

4 lobster tails

100ml white wine

300g macaroni

750ml milk

1 bay leaf

1 onion

50g pancetta

1 tablespoon olive oil

30g butter

1 garlic clove

60g plain flour

1 teaspoon mustard powder

75g Gruyère, grated

75g mature Cheddar, grated

50g breadcrumbs

There are many reasons I love visiting Maine and Massachusetts every summer, but the main one is lobster mac 'n' cheese! We're lucky that Peter's dad sets lobster creels near our hut, so I've brought this great recipe back to Scotland with me.

METHOD

Simmer the lobster tails in a large pan of water, uncovered, for 8 to 10 minutes or until the shells turn bright red. When cooled, separate the lobster meat from the tails and chop into bite-sized chunks.

Add the white wine to a pan and then add the lobster tail shells. Simmer for 5 minutes. Strain to keep the wine.

Preheat the oven to 180°C/360°F.

Cook your macaroni in salted boiling water for 8 minutes, or until nearly al dente. Drain.

Simmer the milk, bay leaf and a slice of onion slowly for 5 minutes, then carefully sieve to retain the flavoured milk. Set aside.

Fry the rest of the onion and pancetta in oil and butter. Stir in the garlic, flour and mustard powder then, a ladleful at a time, add your sieved milk, stirring to combine until all the milk has been used and you have a thick sauce. Pour in the wine that you simmered the lobsters in and add two-thirds of your cheese.

Now, add your cooked macaroni, lobster and sauce to a casserole dish, sprinkle over your breadcrumbs and the rest of the cheese. Place in the oven for 35 minutes until the topping is toasty brown.

PEARL BARLEY RISOTTO WITH BLACK PUDDING CROUTONS

INGREDIENTS

Knob of butter

100g pancetta

1 onion

1 leek

1 courgette

200g pearl barley

150ml white wine

1.25 litres chicken or vegetable stock, easy to make at home but stock cubes are fine too

150g frozen peas

1 tablespoon crème fraîche

30g Parmesan

2 slices of black pudding

Known in Gaelic as *Marag Dhubh*, Stornoway Black Pudding is made from beef suet, oatmeal, onion, blood, salt and pepper. The most famous (and my favourite) is from Charles MacLeod Butchers in Stornoway, locally known as Charlie Barleys. Their original farm was at Crobeag; the croft house I was born in overlooked Crobeag, which makes this recipe even more special to me.

METHOD

In a casserole pot heat the butter over a medium heat, fry the pancetta until nearly crispy. Chop your onion, leek and courgette then add them to the pan and sauté for 5 minutes until they have softened.

Add the pearl barley to the pot and stir to combine. Pour in the white wine and cook for a minute or so until the liquid has reduced.

Add the stock to the pot and leave to simmer for 35 to 40 minutes, stirring occasionally until the pearl barley is tender. The consistency should be creamy and a little loose. Take off the heat and stir in the frozen peas, crème fraîche and grated Parmesan.

Before serving, preheat the oven to 200°C/400°F. Then chop the black pudding into crouton-sized chunks. Spread the black pudding out evenly across a baking tray and roast for 5 to 6 minutes.

Serve in bowls with the black pudding croutons sprinkled over the warm, creamy risotto.

SEÒRAS
& SONGS

You have one new message:

Hello, this is BBC Alba. We are filming a documentary about Gaelic singers who will be performing at this year's Royal National Mòd and we'd love you to be part of the programme. Call me back if you are interested . . . Bye.

It was the 17th of September 2016 and four weeks until I was to perform on stage for the Silver Pendant at the Royal National Mòd in Stornoway. The Mòd is like the Eurovision Song Contest of Gaelic music, just replace the sequins with kilts and fireworks with cèilidh dancing. Since it began in 1892, this annual music contest has tested singers, dancers and musicians in a number of competitions – and more importantly tests the livers of the performers at the many cèilidhs every evening in the pubs around the host city. Singing in Gaelic and drinking whisky very much go hand in hand!

Each autumn a Scottish town plays host to two thousand Gaelic performers from across the world, and that year Stornoway would be host for the sixth time. I was working in London at the time, and I was excited to be heading home to the island, so when I called the BBC back, I agreed to be part of the programme. The weeks went by quickly and the four songs I needed to perform began to take shape. I was told that a cameraman called Peter MacQueen would meet me at

Stornoway airport. And as I stepped off the wee plane from Glasgow and walked across the tarmac to arrivals – there stood Peter. We got on from the minute we met and I spent the day in front of the camera recording different sequences for the programme.

Near the end of that day, Peter asked if I minded going to meet with the rest of the production team. As we walked into the offices of Mac TV, a snoozing dog sensed our arrival and awoke in a scurry of barking, postulating and excitement. 'This is Seòras,' said Peter. But despite our introductions, Seòras continued to act like I was an enemy invader here to snatch away Peter.

Trying to make a good impression, I smiled and went to pat Seòras on the nose. As I bent down, he turned on his heels and scampered behind Peter with his nose in the air, leaving me with my hand eleven inches above the carpet where Seòras had been. At that moment, I didn't know what breed of dog he was. I had grown up on the croft with Border collies as sheep dogs. To be honest, I never even knew other dog breeds existed until the first time I left the island.

So, I asked, innocently enough, 'What kind of dog is she?'

'HE is a Westie,' was Peter's reply.

And this was the day that Peter and Seòras MacQueen walked (and barked) into my life.

I went on to learn that Peter and Seòras both hail from the same county of Scotland, Argyllshire. West Highland White Terriers were first bred by Colonel Edward Donald Malcolm who was the 16th Laird of Poltalloch. Colonel Malcolm is believed to have decided to only keep white terriers after an unfortunate accident where he shot his favourite dog when he mistook it for a fox – and those white dogs he bred are the ancestors of Seòras and all Westies worldwide.

The Poltalloch estate is only about fifteen miles as the crow flies from our hut, where Peter and I spend time living 'off-grid' and there is nowhere in the world that Seòras feels more at home than on the shorelines of Clachan-Seil.

Like most Westies, their character means they are very devoted to one person, so it took me some time to be accepted into Seòras' circle of trust. But after months of walks, sitting

on my knee as we drove through Scotland, and evenings at my feet in the kitchen as he waited, ever hopeful, that a piece of roast chicken would fall to the floor, he finally saw me as a member of the family.

Since then, the three of us are rarely apart and Seòras always wants to be involved in everything we do – out on the canoe, climbing hills, planting vegetables, but especially together in front of the wood-burning stove every evening.

It's taken a couple of years, but when Peter and Seòras arrive home in the evening, Seòras scampers through the house to find me, wagging his tail, looking for a pat on the nose. Even though I know his inner monologue is actually saying, 'Right, Coinneach, where's my dinner?' I pretend for that split second he is pleased to see me, just for me – not my roast chicken.

So, that year at the Mòd, as my name was called, I walked onto the stage with the pleats of my kilt swirling behind me and I looked out to the audience. I had reached the final of the Silver Pendant competition. I could see Peter behind his camera giving me a supportive smile as I began to perform the Nova Scotian lament *A' Choille Ghruamach*. As I finished the final sombre verse, the judges looked up from their scorecards in the front row and smiled warmly as the audience cheered. I returned to my seat and nervously awaited the results.

But there was no fairy-tale ending to Peter's TV programme . . . I would finish second. But still, I would return a year later to win the Silver Pendant. This time Peter would be in the audience without his TV camera, but instead supporting me from the sidelines. Our passion for Gaelic singing continued and the following year again, Peter and I won the National Mòd performing as a duet with another Canadian Gaelic song *Tàladh Na Beinne Guirme*.

Since then, we have sung on stages as far and wide as Oban and New York. And now we perform together as *Gillean Challainn*, the Hogmanay Boys, singing traditional Gaelic songs and telling stories.

So, that day in Stornoway did change my life in ways I could never have expected, and I'm very lucky that Peter and Seòras continue to be such a special part of it.

SEÒRAS & SONGS

5
WEE TREATS

'S fheàrr am bonnach beag le beannachd, na am bonnach mòr le mallachd.

Better the wee scone with a blessing, than the big scone with a curse.

HEATHER BISCOTTI

INGREDIENTS

90g whole almonds

40g whole hazelnuts

355g plain flour

1½ teaspoons baking
powder

Pinch of salt

105g caster sugar

150g light brown sugar

3 eggs

½ teaspoon almond extract

85g olive oil

1 heaped teaspoon dried
heather flowers

½ orange, zested

This recipe is from Amanda who runs the Temple, a beautiful café in Northton on the Isle of Harris. Bringing a Scottish twist to these Italian baked biscuits . . . maybe we should call them Biscotty?!

This recipe calls for dried heather. To create this, simply cut spikes of flowers while they are still in bud, then hang them to dry in small bunches out of direct sunlight.

METHOD

Preheat the oven to 160°C/320°F.

Place all the nuts on a tray and into the oven for 5 minutes just to toast them a little, then let them cool.

Add the nuts to a bowl along with the flour, baking powder, salt, both kinds of sugar and stir together.

Blend together the eggs, almond extract and olive oil then add half the heather flowers and half the orange zest and stir together.

Add the dry to the wet ingredients and mix until well combined – it will be a sticky dough.

Let it sit in the bowl for about 10 minutes; this helps to make it more manageable to shape. Line a baking tray with parchment paper.

Wet your hands (if you don't the mix will stick to them). Roll the dough into logs, each approximately 25cm long. Place on the lined baking tray and sprinkle with the remaining heather flowers and orange zest.

Put it in the oven for about 20 minutes until golden brown. Remove from the oven and allow to cool.

Turn the oven down to 150°C/300°F.

After 10 minutes of cooling, slice the biscotti on the diagonal into 12cm slices. Return the tray to the oven and bake for another 5 minutes, turn over and continue to bake for another 5 minutes until golden brown. Place them on a wire rack to cool and then keep them in an airtight Kilner jar.

MILLIONAIRE'S SHORTBREAD

INGREDIENTS

For the shortbread

200g butter

100g sugar

275g plain flour

For the caramel

397g condensed milk

200g butter

3 tablespoons sugar

4 tablespoons golden syrup

For the topping

250g milk chocolate

With its classic shortbread base, thick caramel middle and extravagant chocolate top, you'll find millionaire's shortbread for sale in every café around Scotland – and we are all very grateful for that!

METHOD

Preheat your oven to 180°C/350°F.

Cream your butter and sugar together, then mix in the flour until you form a dough. Line a 23cm x 23cm tin with baking parchment.

Firmly press the mixture into the bottom of the tin and bake in the oven for 20 minutes or until it's a pale golden colour. Leave in the tin to cool.

In a large saucepan pour in the condensed milk, butter, sugar and golden syrup and melt on a medium heat until the sugar has dissolved – be sure to keep stirring constantly.

Once the sugar has dissolved, turn the heat up high. As soon as it's boiling – then you must stir constantly and vigorously! Between 2 to 3 minutes should be enough to create a thicker caramel with a slightly darker golden colour.

Pour the caramel onto the shortbread base and leave to set for an hour in the fridge. Take it out 15 minutes before you plan to pour over your chocolate.

Break up the chocolate, add half to a bowl and place in the microwave in bursts of 20 seconds until melted, then add the rest of the chocolate and stir until completely melted. Cover the caramel with a layer of chocolate and place back in the fridge for an hour to set. Remove from the fridge, dip a sharp knife in hot water, slice into chunky bars and serve.

CUSTARD CREAMS

(MAKES 8 TO 12 BISCUITS)

INGREDIENTS

170g butter

55g icing sugar

170g self-raising flour

55g custard powder

For the filling

50g butter

20g custard powder

80g icing sugar

There is something very rewarding about mastering a classic biscuit recipe like these beloved custard creams. The buttery biscuit and creamy, custardy middle make them perfect to dunk in your cuppa! The number of biscuits this recipe makes depends on the size of your biscuit cutter.

METHOD

Preheat your oven to 180°C/350°F. Lightly grease a baking tray with butter.

In a large bowl, cream the butter and icing sugar. Add the flour and custard powder a wee bit at a time until it forms a paste.

Now roll this into tablespoon-sized balls, place onto your greased baking tray and press each ball down lightly with a fork.

Bake for 12 to 14 minutes and then allow to cool.

To make your filling, mix together the butter, custard powder and icing sugar to create a butter cream.

Spread this thickly onto half the biscuits and sandwich together.

MACAROONS

INGREDIENTS

110g potatoes

1 teaspoon vanilla essence

450g icing sugar

150g shredded coconut

200g dark chocolate

Don't mix these up with French macarons! These traditional Scottish treats are made with a special ingredient – mashed potatoes! It makes a wonderful fondant centre, and what's more no one will ever guess your secret . . .

METHOD

Peel and boil your potatoes in water until tender. Drain your potatoes and allow them to dry out before mashing them.

Once the mashed potato is completely cool, add your vanilla and then begin to add your icing sugar a tablespoon at a time; each time stir until combined. It will start out runny but begin to thicken up as you add more icing sugar.

Line a freezer-proof dish with baking paper. Transfer the fondant mixture into it and spread it out evenly. Freeze for 2 hours.

Remove from the freezer, slice into bite-sized squares and then shape them into wee balls with your hands. Place them back on the baking paper and freeze for a further 2 hours.

Preheat the oven to 160°C/320°F and place 75g of the shredded coconut on a baking tray lined with baking paper. Allow the coconut to toast and brown, which should take about 8 minutes. Give the tray a good shake halfway through.

Mix the toasted coconut together with the untoasted coconut in a bowl.

Break up the chocolate, add half to a bowl and place in the microwave in bursts of 20 seconds until melted, then add the rest of the chocolate and stir until completely melted.

When the chocolate is melted, remove the balls from the freezer. Dip each one into the chocolate then roll it in the coconut. This is very messy work!

Place the coated balls on a wire rack and place in the fridge for an hour before serving.

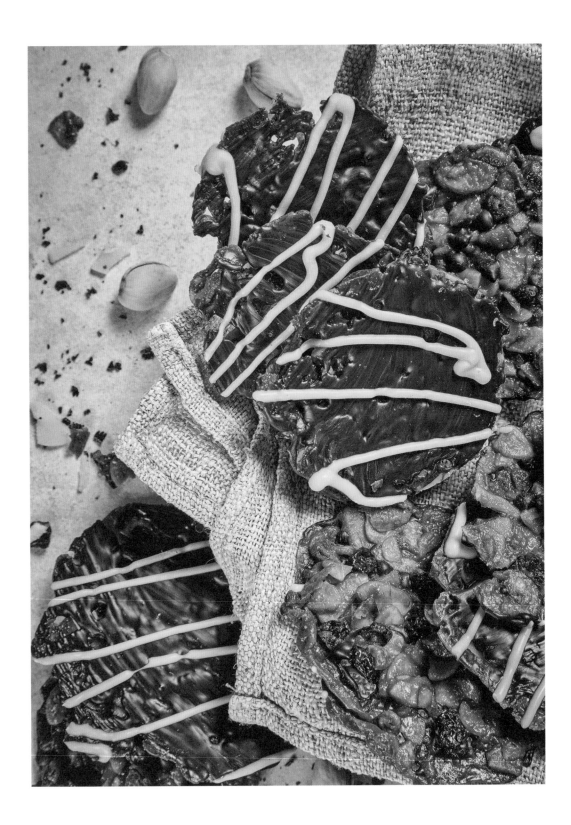

FLORENTINES

INGREDIENTS

30g pistachios, unsalted

30g glacé cherries

30g currants

30g dried cranberries

60g flaked almonds

20g plain flour

50g butter

70g dark brown sugar

2 tablespoons double cream

Pinch of salt

200g dark chocolate

50g white chocolate

Packed with cherries, dried fruit, pistachios and almonds, these chocolate-dipped Florentines make the ideal wee treat. Watch them carefully as they bake, and allow them plenty room on the baking tray to make sure they cook evenly to give a crisp biscuit.

METHOD

Preheat the oven to 180°C/350°F.

Chop the pistachios and glacé cherries roughly, then mix with the rest of the dried fruit and almonds in a bowl. Sift in the flour over them to coat them evenly.

Melt the butter and sugar together slowly in a pan. Take the pan off the heat and stir in the cream and salt. Pour over the fruit and nuts then combine.

Line a baking tray with greaseproof paper and place teaspoonfuls of the Florentine mixture onto it. Space them out well and bake for about 10 minutes. Let them cool on the tray before transferring to a wire rack.

Microwave the dark chocolate for 20 seconds, stir, then heat in 10 second bursts until melted.

Use a pastry brush to coat half of the cooled Florentines with the chocolate. Be sure to let the first layer set before adding a second.

Finally melt the white chocolate (as above) and drizzle in patterns over the dark chocolate.

HIELAN' COOS

(MAKES 8 TO 10 CUPCAKES)

INGREDIENTS

For the cupcakes

100g plain flour

20g cocoa powder

140g sugar

1½ teaspoons baking
powder

Pinch of salt

40g butter, at room
temperature

120ml milk

1 egg

¼ teaspoon vanilla extract

For the decoration

100g milk chocolate

200g butter, softened

400g icing sugar

5 tablespoons cocoa
powder

Pinch of salt

2 tablespoons milk

50g white fondant icing

50g pink fondant icing

1 packet of fondant
googly eyes

My god-daughter Gabrielle loves visiting the Highland cows at her local farm and that's why we have made these wee Hielan' Coos. Cute chocolate cupcakes that are loved by all kids (and adults)!

METHOD

Heat the oven to 180°C/350°F. Line a muffin tin with paper cases.

Place the flour, cocoa powder, sugar, baking powder, a pinch of salt and the butter in a bowl and whisk together until combined.

Next, whisk the milk, egg and vanilla extract together in a jug, then slowly pour about half into the flour-based mixture and blend together. Once combined, add the remaining liquid and continue mixing for a couple more minutes until the mixture is smooth, but be careful not to over mix.

Spoon about 2 tablespoons of the cupcake mixture into each case. Bake for 20 minutes until a skewer comes out clean.

Leave the cupcakes in the tray for 2 to 3 minutes before turning out onto a wire rack to cool.

Now make the decoration. Break up the chocolate, add half to a bowl and place in the microwave in bursts of 20 seconds until melted, then add the rest of the chocolate and stir until completely melted. Leave the melted chocolate to cool for a couple of minutes.

Cream the butter and icing sugar together. Sift in the cocoa powder and pour in the melted chocolate, a pinch of salt and the milk, then mix again until smooth.

To decorate, cover each cupcake with a layer of the buttercream. Roll out a 6cm piece of white fondant icing to create the horns. With your pink fondant icing, create a 1cm oval shape and place 2 dots for the nose and a line for the mouth. Add these to the top of the cupcake and then place on 2 googly eyes.

Put the rest of the buttercream into a piping bag with a thin tip to create the hair. Pipe the hair down from the top of the cupcake in straggly lines. *Moo!*

CHOCOLATE GINGER SNAPS WITH LEMON CURD

(MAKES 20 BISCUITS)

INGREDIENTS

175g plain flour

50g butter

1 teaspoon ground ginger

½ teaspoon bicarbonate of soda

90g soft brown sugar

2 tablespoons golden syrup

1 small egg

150g lemon curd, homemade is always best!

150g dark chocolate

The fiery ginger, zesty lemon and dark chocolate combine perfectly to create these biscuits. They take a wee bit of patience to assemble but your guests will appreciate it.

METHOD

Preheat the oven to 180°C/350°F.

Put the flour, butter, ground ginger and bicarbonate of soda in a mixing bowl and combine.

Add the sugar, golden syrup and egg, mix well until it forms a firm pastry mix.

Roll out the dough on a floured surface to about 5mm thick. Use a cookie cutter to create your biscuit shapes, place on a greased baking tray and into the oven for 7 minutes or until golden. Allow to cool on a wire rack.

Once cooled, dip one side of the ginger snap into the lemon curd, place them back on the wire rack and put in the fridge to set for 30 minutes.

Break up the chocolate, add half to a bowl and place in the microwave in bursts of 20 seconds until melted, then add the rest of the chocolate and stir until completely melted. Let it cool slightly, then dip the same side as the lemon curd and leave to set.

CHOCOLATE HONEYCOMB

INGREDIENTS

200g golden caster sugar

5 tablespoons golden syrup

2 teaspoons bicarbonate of
soda

350g dark chocolate

Making honeycomb is like a magic trick, and these wee chocolate-covered treats make the perfect festive gift. If you can bear to be parted from them, that is!

METHOD

Line a 20cm square tin with parchment paper.

Add the sugar and golden syrup to a deep saucepan and place over a low heat until the sugar has melted. Then turn up the heat and simmer until the caramel has an amber colour (this should only take a minute).

Then, as quickly as you can, take off the heat, tip in the bicarbonate of soda and beat with a whisk or wooden spoon. The caramel will begin to foam. Pour into the prepared tin immediately and leave to cool.

After an hour in the tin, the honeycomb should be cooled and hard.

Break up the chocolate, add half to a bowl and place in the microwave in bursts of 20 seconds until melted, then add the rest of the chocolate and stir until completely melted.

With a rolling pin, bang the honeycomb into chunks and dip each piece into the chocolate. Leave to set on a wire rack – then share and enjoy your crunchie delight!

VANILLA TABLET

INGREDIENTS

450g granulated sugar

250ml milk

1 tablespoon golden syrup

60g butter

1 teaspoon vanilla essence

Scottish tablet is not as soft as fudge, nor is it as hard as toffee. It has a unique and delicious crumbly texture all of its own. The first recipe was discovered in *The Household Book* of Lady Grisell Baillie (1692–1733), and it is still made in kitchens throughout Scotland every week.

METHOD

Grease well a baking tin with a low lip.

Place the sugar, milk and golden syrup into a pan. Now warm over a gentle heat and stir occasionally until all the sugar is dissolved. Once dissolved, add the butter and allow to melt.

Bring the mix slowly to boiling point. Now increase the heat and stir continuously while the mixture boils until it has reached soft-ball stage at 120°C.

Take off the heat and add the vanilla essence.

Beat the mixture until it is almost setting in the pan. Pour the mixture into your prepared baking tin and allow to set.

After 30 minutes, score into wee bite-sized pieces, then once it has completely cooled cut into pieces.

PÒGAN BEAGA

(MAKES A DOZEN CUPCAKES)

INGREDIENTS

For the cupcakes

150g butter

150g sugar

1 teaspoon vanilla essence

3 eggs

150g self-raising flour

½ teaspoon baking powder

For the salted caramel

200g granulated sugar

90g salted butter

120ml double cream

1 teaspoon salt

For the buttercream

250g butter

1 teaspoon vanilla essence

500g icing sugar

For the vanilla tablet

See recipe on page 148

Pògan Beaga is the Gaelic for wee kisses, and whoever you bake these for will definitely be giving you a hug and kiss to say thank you. Topping your salted caramel cupcake is a square of vanilla tablet. This recipe from Tina Campbell, a fantastic island baker, will give you a real sugar rush!

METHOD

Preheat the oven to 180°C/350°F. Line a muffin tin with paper cases.

To make the cupcakes, cream together the butter, sugar and vanilla for a few minutes until light and fluffy. Then whisk in one egg at a time until fully incorporated.

Sieve in the flour and baking powder and fold in until all combined

Spoon in the mix so your cupcake cases are two-thirds full.

Bake for 17 minutes or until they are golden brown and spring back when you press the top. Allow them to cool on a wire rack.

Now make the salted caramel. Heat the granulated sugar in a saucepan slowly, stirring constantly until it turns into an amber liquid. Stir in the butter. Once the butter has melted and combined, simmer for a minute without stirring.

A bit at a time, stir in the cream. Once it has combined, allow to bubble for a minute. Remove from the heat and stir in the salt. While you are waiting for it to cool, it will begin to thicken.

Next make the buttercream. Cream the butter with a hand mixer for 3 to 5 minutes until really pale and fluffy. Then add the vanilla and then blend in the icing sugar in batches.

To assemble the cupcakes, use a teaspoon to hollow out some of the centre of the cupcake and add a spoon of salted caramel. Pipe the buttercream on top, drizzle with a little caramel and top with tablet.

CHEVIOTS & LOOMS

When my grandfather, Dòmhnall Sheumais, was born on the 28th September 1879, his mother Christina and father Seumas were living in a Blackhouse in the coastal village of Marvig on the Isle of Lewis. Their home, built with stone walls, roofed with turf and thatch, would have sheltered not only the family but also their two cows. All warmed against the storms rolling in from the Atlantic by a peat fire in a central open hearth with the smoke filtering out through the thatched straw roof.

Marvig comes from the Old Norse *Maravik* meaning 'Sea Bay' and so it was appropriate that, like many men from the village, my grandfather spent most of his working life at sea. When he married my Granny Ann, he was already forty-seven years old. And when his youngest daughter, my mam, was born, he was sixty-three.

Ciorstaidh Anna – my mam – was brought up with her four siblings Seumas, Shonnie, Kenny and Louisa in the old family home in Marvig. Her father died when she was a teenager. And, at a young age, she was tasked with finding work. Her brothers, Seumas and Shonnie, like their father, had gone to sea. Her sister Louisa worked as the postwoman, delivering the mail to all the houses around their village of Marvig and nearby Calbost. But many women from the island, including my mother, had to seek work on the mainland. There they were popular because

of their strong work ethic and warm disposition. My mother worked as a nanny and in hotels in Glasgow, but she missed home so much, she told her family she wanted to return.

But beyond crofting and the subsistence it provided in return for endless hard work, there were few career opportunities on Lewis in the 1950s and '60s, particularly for women. There was, though, one extraordinary exception to this rule. It involved a product with a name that resonated around the world. And so Ciorstaidh Anna and her older brother Kenny would get up every morning, walk the few steps from the house across their croft to a shed. In there stood two Hattersley looms where they would spend their days weaving Harris Tweed.

It is difficult to overstate how integral Harris Tweed has been to the fabric – social, cultural, economic – of the islands. Weaving was the work that kept people going through the hardest of times. Walking through Cromore as a child, like every other Lewis and Harris village, the noise that broke the still of a summer's day or competed with the gales in winter was the rhythmic clacking of Hattersley looms, producing a cloth that would end up on the catwalks of Paris or in the department stores of New York.

Every luxury brand in the world would give its right arm for the kind of story that lies behind Harris Tweed. For, in order to bear its famous name, our island fabric – the same one my mother wove, and generations of my family before her – must be made from pure virgin wool, handwoven at the home of the weaver in the Outer Hebrides of Scotland. All stages of the process – at the mill before it goes to the weaver and finishing when it returns – must also be carried out in the islands.

Though the islands that produce Harris Tweed might seem remote to many, our fabric has been worn by icons of our time. In the post-war years, the Harris Tweed blazer became an essential item in the wardrobe of every well-dressed, prosperous American. These wardrobes included those of John F. Kennedy who bought all his suits and jackets from Chipp Inc., one of the pioneers of the so-called Ivy Look to which Harris Tweed was integral.

But it is another US President who is most synonymous with the brand of Harris Tweed: Dwight Eisenhower. In the 1950s, so as to support US producers, President Eisenhower came under pressure to impose tariffs on all imported fabrics. On hearing this, a delegation from the Isle of Lewis took the long journey across the Atlantic to Washington DC to plead before the US Federal Trade Commission for Harris Tweed to not have this levy placed upon them.

The delegation was led by the Free Church of Scotland minister, Reverend Murdoch MacRae. He told the Commission that the Hebrides, 'had raised a hardy, courageous and loyal race of men and women' who had 'given a good account of themselves in peace and war'. In fact, during the Second World War, thousands of American lives had been saved by the rescue planes based on the islands. MacRae told his rapt audience that he did not want 'to see again the people of these islands being scattered to the ends of the earth, but that was what would happen if their industry failed'. Eisenhower – who himself had strong Scottish connections – and the political might of Washington relented and now, right up to the present day, Harris Tweed retains its privileged status in all US trade agreements.

Every spring heralds a new cycle of creativity as the changing island landscapes inspire the colours and patterns designed by Harris Tweed Hebrides. Their goal has been to put 'a new twist to an old yarn'. The drive from Cromore to their mill in Shawbost on the west side of the island takes me past the lochs and through the villages where the crofters and

their border collies gather sheep on the hills.

The journey to make Harris Tweed begins when those crofters shear their sheep. And when I arrive at the mill in Shawbost, a batch of Cheviot wool is just being delivered. Waving from the door is Margaret Ann, whose family is steeped in the traditions of Harris Tweed. As she takes me around the mill, I share her strong sense of pride and identity for this unique and wonderful Hebridean industry.

I see the wool being blended, spun and warped at the mill. The warp is wound onto beams and each day (except Sunday, of course!) the Harris Tweed Hebrides lorry sets off to deliver the beams to the weavers. When it reaches his or her home, the first painstaking task is to 'tie in' 1,400 individual warp threads to the loom, all in a regimented order set by designers at the mill. Then the weav-

ing begins, at all hours of day and night, just as it was in the days of my mother and Uncle Kenny.

One final act is performed at the mill in Shawbost. When the tweed returns from the homes of the weavers, the Harris Tweed Authority Inspector has the special role of authenticating each metre by bestowing upon it the Orb trademark – the country's oldest trademark and the ultimate seal of approval.

The looms are quieter now and there are fewer of them. But the importance of Harris Tweed is undiminished. It is something I am very proud of – that my family is part of the history of Harris Tweed. And as I wave farewell to Margaret Ann, I clip Seòras into his new Harris Tweed collar and together we set off over the hills back home to Cromore.

6
CRUMBLES & PUDDINGS

Is olc an còcaire nach imlich a mheur

It's a poor cook who doesn't lick his finger.

CALEDONIAN FOREST GÂTEAU

INGREDIENTS

For the sponge

175g butter

200g golden caster sugar

3 eggs

1 teaspoon vanilla paste

100g dark chocolate, melted

200g self-raising flour

2 tablespoons cocoa
   powder

½ teaspoon bicarbonate of
   soda

150g soured cream

For the filling and
decoration

100g raspberry jam

400g fresh raspberries

75ml Chambord

500ml double cream

100g dark chocolate,
   coarsely grated

Inspired by the traditional Black Forest gâteau – with its layers of chocolate sponge, cream and boozy cherries – this Scottish version replaces cherries and kirsch with raspberries and Chambord, a delicious and decadent French raspberry liqueur.

METHOD

Preheat the oven to 180°C/350°F. You will need 3 greased and lined 18cm cake tins.

With a hand mixer, cream the butter and sugar until pale and fluffy. Beat in the eggs, one at a time, then the vanilla, the melted chocolate, flour, cocoa powder and bicarbonate of soda until combined. Finally, beat in the soured cream.

Divide the batter between the 3 prepared tins and bake for 20 to 25 minutes or until a skewer comes out of the cake clean. Cool the cakes in the tins for 5 minutes, then turn out onto a wire rack to cool completely.

For the filling, put the jam in a saucepan with 200g of fresh raspberries and 25ml of Chambord and place over a low heat. Bring to a simmer and stir frequently for 6 to 8 minutes. Leave to cool and thicken for 15 minutes.

Whip the double cream with an electric hand-whisk until soft peaks form. Place 300ml of it in a separate bowl and chop 50g of the raspberries and gently stir them into the cream.

Brush the cooled cakes with 25ml of the Chambord before placing the first sponge on a plate. Spread on a thick layer of the jam mixture. Place the second sponge on top and add a thick layer of the raspberry-filled cream. Add the final sponge on top and cover with a thin layer of the raspberry-filled cream.

With the leftover cream, put a thin layer all around the outside of the cake, then pipe the rest into swirls around the top of the cake.

Cover the top of the cake with the rest of the fresh raspberries and brush them with the leftover Chambord. Finally, with your hands, press the grated chocolate gently around the side of the cake. Serve.

STICKY TOFFEE PUDDING

(MAKES 6 MINI PUDS)

INGREDIENTS

For the pudding

200g dates

200ml hot black tea

1 teaspoon bicarbonate of
soda

80g butter

2 tablespoons black treacle

50g muscovado sugar

2 eggs

150g plain flour

2 teaspoons baking powder

For the sauce

150g butter

300g muscovado sugar

1 tablespoon black treacle

200ml double cream

There are no three words in the English language more beautiful than 'sticky toffee pudding'; okay, maybe 'I love you' comes a close second! This is an indulgent pud that will make a weekend lunch with family end perfectly.

METHOD

Chop up your dates and pour your hot black tea over them, then stir in the bicarbonate of soda and leave for 30 minutes.

Preheat your oven to 160°C/320°F.

Cream your butter and black treacle together. Then add your sugar, eggs, flour and baking powder and mix well.

Once cooled, mash the dates into the tea and add to the batter.

Combine and spoon evenly into a greased muffin tin tray and bake for 20 minutes, until risen and firm.

To make the sauce, add the butter, sugar and black treacle to a pan and simmer until the sugar has dissolved and the butter melted. Then turn up the heat and let it bubble for a minute or so to create a dark toffee-coloured sauce. Take it off the heat and stir in the cream.

Serve warm with the pudding covered in the toffee sauce and a big scoop of vanilla ice cream.

MARMALADE BREAD & BUTTER PUDDING

INGREDIENTS

35g dried cranberries

2 tablespoons whisky

8 slices of thick white bread

1 tablespoon of butter and
    marmalade for each
    sandwich

For the custard filling

1 egg

2 egg yolks

1½ tablespoons sugar

300ml double cream

50ml milk

½ teaspoon vanilla extract

1 tablespoon brown sugar

Bread and butter pudding was first described in Eliza Smith's *The Compleat Housewife* written in 1727 – and it is still a household favourite across Scotland. It's often recommended to use bread that is going stale as it soaks up more of the lovely custard! The addition of cranberries and marmalade balances the sweetness of the pudding perfectly. You might like to use homemade marmalade in this recipe (see page 21).

METHOD

Preheat your oven to 180°C/350°F.

Soak the cranberries in your whisky and let them rest for 30 minutes. Then with your bread, make butter and marmalade sandwiches. Cut into triangles and arrange in a pattern of pointy side up, pointy side down in your oven dish and scatter your whisky-soaked cranberries on top.

Now make the custardy filling. Whisk your eggs and sugar together, then add your cream, milk and vanilla. Once combined, slowly pour over the sandwiches. Scatter brown sugar on top and leave to set for 15 minutes, before putting in the oven for 35 to 40 minutes.

Serve warm with homemade custard (see page 173) or ice cream. Or even both!

HARRIS GIN & RASPBERRY PAVLOVA

INGREDIENTS

For the meringue

6 egg whites

375g sugar

2½ teaspoons cornflour

For the sauce

300g fresh raspberries

100ml Harris Gin (or your gin of choice!)

4 tablespoons sugar

For the topping

600ml double cream

500g bag of frozen mixed berries (allow time for these to defrost)

For this recipe, it's best to make the meringue in advance and, just before serving, add the layers of cream and fruit – it's a dessert that always gets a gasp from dinner guests as it arrives at the table. Serve with a gin & tonic!

METHOD

Place the fresh raspberries for the sauce in a bowl, pour over the gin and leave to steep.

Preheat the oven to 180°C/350°F.

Now make the meringue. Whisk the egg whites until satiny peaks form, then whisk in the sugar a tablespoon at a time. Sprinkle the cornflour over the meringue and gently fold until thoroughly mixed in.

Line a baking tray with baking parchment and spoon the meringue into a 20cm round in the centre.

Place in the oven, then immediately turn the temperature down to 150°C/300°F and cook for an hour. Switch off the oven, open the oven door fully and leave the pavlova to cool.

While the meringue cools, make the raspberry gin sauce by adding the steeped berries and gin liquid to a saucepan. Add the sugar and set over a low heat, stirring gently, until the raspberries begin to break up and the sugar has fully dissolved, then set aside to cool.

It's easy to pick up a bag of frozen mixed berries, usually with raspberries, blackberries, blackcurrants and redcurrants, which is perfect for this recipe. Defrost the berries in a bowl and stir in half of the raspberry gin sauce.

Meanwhile, add the double cream to a clean bowl and whisk until soft peaks form. Spoon this whipped cream over the meringue, and then top the pavlova with the mixed fruit. Finally drizzle over the remaining raspberry gin sauce. Serve immediately.

FIG & GINGER CRUMBLE

INGREDIENTS

5 figs

Cup of hot ginger tea

150g rolled oats

Handful of cashews,
    chopped

150g golden caster sugar

70g plain flour

175g butter, melted

2 tablespoons golden syrup

4 pears, chopped

3cm chunk of fresh ginger

The fresh ginger does something very special to the figs in this warming autumnal crumble. The fiery heat of the ginger complements the soft fruit and oaty topping so well. Just make sure you've perfected my homemade custard recipe (on page 173) to pour on top.

METHOD

Slice your figs into bitesize chunks and soak in hot ginger tea for 15 minutes.

Preheat your oven to 175°C/350°F. Choose your bowls – the crumble works equally well in a family-sized pudding bowl or about 4 individual bowls.

To make your crumble topping, add your oats, chopped cashews, 100g of the sugar and the flour to a bowl and then stir in the melted butter and golden syrup.

Drain your figs and add them to a bowl, along with the chopped pears. Grate your ginger on top and cover with the remaining 50g of sugar and stir together. Then cover with your oaty crumble.

Place in the oven for 35 minutes or until golden brown and bubbling. Serve warm with homemade custard.

HOMEMADE VANILLA CUSTARD

INGREDIENTS

1 vanilla pod

50g sugar

2 egg yolks

1 teaspoon cornflour

150ml double cream

150ml milk

If you want to make me happy, pour gravy over my roast dinner and custard over my pudding. Simple! It doesn't really matter what is underneath! This vanilla custard recipe is perfect to pour on crumbles, sponges and puddings.

METHOD

Slice the vanilla pod and scrape out the vanilla seeds.

In a bowl, whisk together your sugar and egg yolks until shiny and pale. Add the cornflour and whisk again.

Into a saucepan, add your cream, milk and vanilla seeds along with the pod. Simmer but take off the heat before it boils and remove the pod.

Whisking constantly, pour a wee bit of the hot milk over the egg mixture. Keep adding a wee bit at a time and stir until it is all combined.

Place this back on a low heat, stirring constantly for 5 to 7 minutes.

You know it's ready when you can draw a clear line through the custard on the back of a spoon. You want it thick but still pourable.

APPLE AMARETTI CRUMBLE

INGREDIENTS

500g cooking apples

Pinch of salt

175g soft brown sugar

½ teaspoon cinnamon

175g butter

2 tablespoons golden syrup

50g amaretti biscuits

150g rolled oats

70g plain flour

The Italian word *amaro* means bitter, and as these wee biscuits are flavoured with bitter almonds, they were called *amaretti* – literally the little bitter ones. They complement the sweetness of the flapjack crumble and soft fruit in this family favourite.

METHOD

Preheat the oven to 170°C/340°F. Choose whether you want to make this in a family-sized pudding bowl or about 4 individual bowls.

Peel, core and chop your apples into chunks, cover with a pinch of salt, 50g of your sugar and the cinnamon. Mix together and layer into your chosen bowls.

Gently warm the butter and syrup in a pan until the butter melts.

Meanwhile, in another bowl, crush the amaretti biscuits, not into crumbs but different sized pieces. Add your oats, flour, the remaining 125g of sugar and then stir in your melted butter and golden syrup.

Cover your layer of fruit in the flapjack crumble and place in the oven for 35 minutes or until golden brown and bubbling. Serve warm with homemade custard (see page 173) and/or ice cream!

BRAMBLE BÀRR

(SERVES 2)

INGREDIENTS

100g sugar

3 tablespoons bramble jelly,
see page 32 (or you can
use blackberry jam)

150ml whisky

½ lemon, juiced

1 lemon, with the rind cut into
strips

450ml double cream

200g blackberries

Bàrr is the Gaelic for cream. This layered wild blackberry cream infused
with whisky should be served in glasses to showcase its beautiful colours.

METHOD

Put the sugar, bramble jelly and 100ml of the whisky into a saucepan. Add
the lemon juice and 2 strips of lemon rind. Stir over a medium heat until the
sugar has dissolved and the jelly has melted. Bring to the boil, then allow to
bubble for a minute. Remove from the heat and leave to cool in the pan for
an hour and then remove the rinds.

Add the double cream to a bowl along with the remaining whisky and
whisk until soft peaks form.

Keep a blackberry per glass to decorate the top, then add the rest to a
bowl and crush them gently with a fork.

To assemble, pour a layer of the syrup in the bottom of each glass, then
a layer of whisky cream. Next add a layer of the crushed blackberries,
another layer of cream, a second layer of syrup and a final layer of cream.
Garnish with a blackberry and serve.

VEGAN RICE PUDDING WITH RHUBARB COMPOTE

(SERVES 1 VERY HUNGRY BEAR)

INGREDIENTS

For the rice pudding

100g pudding rice

600ml coconut milk

60g sugar

½ teaspoon mixed spice

Pinch of nutmeg

For the compote

100g rhubarb

½ an orange

20g sugar

10ml water

I know I say *homemade is always best* a lot – but honestly, this time, I REALLY mean it! This simple recipe needs just two saucepans and a little bit of time.

METHOD

First, make the rice pudding. Place the rice in a saucepan, then stir in all the other ingredients. Cook on a low simmer for 45 minutes or until the rice is soft. Be sure to stir regularly.

Next, make the compote. Start by chopping the rhubarb into 2cm chunks. Then with a sharp knife remove 2 slices of peel from the orange. Place the rhubarb and orange peel in a saucepan with the sugar and water then simmer with the lid on for 10 to 15 minutes. Stir occasionally. It will be ready when the rhubarb has completely broken down. Discard the orange peel.

Serve the rice pudding in a dessert bowl, adding a big blob of warm rhubarb compote on top.

HEATHER HONEY STEAMED SPONGE

INGREDIENTS

90g heather honey

70g butter

70g sugar

2 eggs

75g self-raising flour

½ teaspoon baking powder

Scottish heather honey is produced from bees who have had access to the heather moors in Scotland. They take the nectar from the heather and convert it into honey. I love Scottish bees! The unique flavour and amber colour of their honey is perfect for this classic steamed sponge. (Make sure you have some string to hand before you start.)

METHOD

Put 2 tablespoons of the honey into a buttered 1-pint (570ml) pudding basin.

Add the butter, sugar, eggs, flour, baking powder and remaining honey into a bowl and blend with a hand-mixer for 2 minutes. Pour the mixture into the pudding basin, on top of the honey.

Lay a piece of baking parchment on top of a sheet of foil, making a large pleat in the middle, to allow the pudding to rise. Cover the pudding basin foil side up, crimp around the sides and secure tightly with string.

Place the basin in a large saucepan filled halfway with boiling water. Allow that to simmer with the lid on for an hour. Keep an eye on the pan and top up the water if necessary.

Once you remove the foil, place the pudding basin upside down on a plate and serve immediately with homemade vanilla custard (see page 173).

STORMS & SPIRITS

They say if you don't like the weather in the Outer Hebrides just wait a minute . . .

Do you remember that song by Crowded House, 'Four Seasons in One Day'? I always wondered if the Finn Brothers had been holidaying in the Hebrides at the time they wrote that. And even on this early May day, there is still a distinct chill in the air as I drive south to the Isle of Harris. Lewis and Harris make up the most northerly and largest of the Hebridean islands, separated not by the sea, but heather-topped hills. Today, our highest mountain, the Clisham, is surrounded by a horseshoe of snowy peaks with tongue-twisting names like Mull bho Dheas, Mulla bho Thuath and Mullach an Langa.

On crofts below, lambing has begun. Hundreds of bright little bleating bundles are appearing at the feet of their often-bewildered mothers. These lambs are one of the real signs that spring is in the air, even if the weather says something different.

With elemental winds, waves and wide skies, a rollercoaster for the senses found among mountain, moor and machair, the islands are immersed in nature. In summer, the days stretch so long that the sun barely dips below the horizon, while months of long winter darkness bring a blanket of stars and dancing aurora high above.

The weather here gives meteorological meaning to the word 'unpredictable', with marine green seas and intense blue skies suddenly giving way to clouds of ominous grey and horizontal rains. And when the storms roll in, we often find ourselves cut off from the rest of the world as ferries stay safely tied at harbour on the mainland and local shop shelves run dry of fresh supplies.

This might be one of the reasons why we have learned the twin skills of self-sufficiency and depending upon one another. Despite the apparent sparsity of souls (at nine people per square kilometre, the Outer Hebrides has the lowest density of people in Scotland), life here continues to be centred around connections to each other and the seemingly simple but often complex concept of community.

Community is first and foremost about people and the bonds forged between them. It is a hard-to-explain feeling of trust and belonging, a quiet collective agreement to take care of each other when needed. On these islands, there is a long history of working together to meet common goals. The age-old island traditions of crofting, fishing, weaving and peat-cutting all exemplify the benefits of mutual cooperation and the modest truth of many hands making light work. Similarly, a shared, deep-rooted culture expressed through the Gaelic language, religion, music and song has tied the people together into a wider, extended family as tough times here were faced as one.

Our villages are many and scattered, but we are a close-knit community, bound by a love of this special place, our traditions, history, language and culture as well as by the confines – and joys – of our unique geography.

After an hour driving through the hills, I arrive in the main village on the island of Harris – Tarbert. The name Tarbert, or *An Tairbeart* in Scottish Gaelic, is derived from the old Norse word for 'draw boat', meaning a place where the land is so narrow that Viking ships could be pulled across two stretches of water.

I open the door of the Isle of Harris Distillery, welcomed by the warmth of a burning peat fire, which is lit daily by the distillery team. There is a bustle of folk – some taking a guided tour, others queuing in the shop with two bottles of Harris Gin glinting in their arms. There is an immediate sense of a *modern Hebrides*, that the distillery has become a catalyst for positive change within the community, bringing a well-needed new vitality and sense of possibility to the island.

Since the mid-1700s, there has been a succession of key trials and tribulations in our Hebridean history, pushing and pulling people from our shores. Thousands of emigrants have departed the islands in search of a better life, leaving their homes and often families behind, to seek the promise of opportunities across the world. From Cape Breton to North Carolina, Patagonia to the Prairies, our men and women have sailed far and found new homes in almost every corner of the world. And with them, they took their clan names, like MacLeod and MacDonald, Morrison and MacLennan, MacKinnon, MacAskill and many more . . .

At that time, in the eighteenth century, the village of Tarbert held less than a handful of houses. The population was settled mainly on the fertile machair lands of the western shores, and on nearby islands like Pabbay, Berneray and Taransay. Here, oats, potatoes and barley were grown, fishing was commonplace, and cattle kept for milk and meat. Harris was ruled by the chiefs of the Clan MacLeod from castles at Dunvegan and Pabbay, a religious centre at Rodel and their hunting grounds in the forests of North Harris.

But, jumping forward through time, by the

1950s, the community of Harris was twice as large as it is now. And a stark, long-term decline in local population continues to this day, as we continue to face acute demographic challenges and our young people leave to seek work and a different kind of life far from our shores.

Opened in 2015, the Isle of Harris Distillery was established to help address this issue, with ambitions to create sustainable employment and support the broader local economy. By taking pride in the creation of spirits and sharing them with the world.

I'm meeting Calum, one of the Storytellers at the distillery to create the cookbook's signature cocktail, the Cèilidh Martini (check out the recipe on page 194!) using the distinctive sugar kelp seaweed-infused Isle of Harris Gin.

After a long exploration of the island's natural botanicals, the distillery eventually decided on sugar kelp seaweed as their defining ingredient to best express the historic ties and affinity with the sea. On an island where flora often struggles to grow and thrive, there is an abundance of this kelp around the shores, which means it can be used sustainably, harvested by hand by local diver Lewis MacKenzie.

But while the distillery's gin is already on sale – its whisky continues to mature. It's not the first time that whisky has been distilled on the islands. The people from Pabbay, a small island off the western coast, could once boast of the *uisge beatha* which flowed from their hidden stills far from the exciseman's eyes.

Now, 170 years later, the first legal dram is being distilled on Harris. Named the *Hearach*, after the Gaelic word for the people of Harris, it will showcase influences from across the island.

The softest of Hebridean water will come from the fast-flowing *Abhainn Cnoc a 'Charrain*, running over the oldest rocks on earth, Lewisian gneiss. And the distillers have been cutting peat by hand at *Cleite Mhòr*, an area of South Harris where peat has been cut for generations. Every drop will have been distilled, matured, and eventually bottled, by local people here on the Isle of Harris.

It sounds, just like the *Hearaich* themselves, as if their malt whisky is a conversation between nature and nurture, with those two powerful parents each influencing the dram in their own unique ways.

As the old saying goes, *today's rain is tomorrow's whisky*. And as I scurry back to my car under the gathering storm clouds, I'm thankful that providence and place have ensured that this vital supply for the island's spirit-making will never run dry. *Slàinte!*

7
SLÀINTE

E ho-ro, Chaluim mhòir, thugainn còmh' rium gu dram,
Null do bhùth Dhòmh'll 'ic Leòid 's gheibh sinn stòpan de leann,
'S nuair a bhios sinn ga òl 's math chòrdas sinn ann,
Bidh ar n-inntinn air ceòl 's cha bhi òrain oirnn gann
Ann am bùth Dhòmh'll 'ic Leòid.

Hey there, Big Calum, come with me for a dram,
Over to Donald MacLeod's pub and we'll get a pint,
And while we're drinking it we'll have a good time.
Our minds will be on music and there'll be no shortage of songs
In Donald MacLeod's pub.

UISGE BEATHA ICE CREAM

INGREDIENTS

300ml double cream

175ml condensed milk

3 tablespoons whisky

1 tablespoon instant espresso
    powder

50g chocolate chips

Uisge Beatha is the Gaelic for whisky, but its literal translation is 'the water of life'. The powerful flavours of the whisky and espresso balance perfectly with the thick chilled cream. Move aside rum and raisin, there is a new boozy ice cream in town!

METHOD

Pour your double cream and condensed milk into a bowl, add your whisky and espresso powder and blend with a hand mixer until it thickens and ribbons appear in the cream. Finally stir in your chocolate chips.

Spoon into a food storage box, seal the lid and freeze overnight.

Take out of the freezer 10 minutes before serving.

THE CÈILIDH MARTINI

INGREDIENTS

2 grapefruits

200g sugar, plus sugar for
the syrup

60ml Isle of Harris Gin

Calum is one of the storytellers at the Harris Distillery and he helped me create this unique cocktail using their Isle of Harris Gin. You need to start prepping your martini a little in advance, but it'll be worth it!

METHOD

To make the grapefruit oleo, first peel the grapefruits in full.

Put the grapefruit peels into a bowl and sprinkle the sugar over the peels. Muddle the peels and sugar. The sugar will dissolve in the oils released by the citrus peel. Once all the peels have been muddled, cover the bowl with a dish towel and leave it for 24 hours, stirring the mixture occasionally.

Once complete, extract the oleo by squeezing the liquid through a muslin or clean kitchen towel. Refrigerate until required.

Now make your grapefruit syrup. Slice the peeled grapefruits in half, juice them and pour the juice through a sieve into a clean saucepan.

For the syrup, we will do a simple 1:1 ratio of juice to sugar, so add the same weight of sugar to juice. Add the sugar to the pan and stir over a medium heat until all the sugar is dissolved. Let it cool and refrigerate.

To assemble

60ml Isle of Harris Gin

5ml grapefruit syrup

5ml grapefruit oleo

Fill a stirring glass with good ice. Add the gin, grapefruit syrup and grapefruit oleo.

Stir for at least 30 seconds, taste and continue stirring, checking every 10 seconds or so until you are happy with the dilution level.

Pour into a chilled martini glass. I like it ungarnished as it fits with the ethos of the drink, but if you prefer you can garnish with a large grapefruit peel. *Slàinte.*

WHISKY TIRAMISU

INGREDIENTS

6 eggs

200g sugar

250g mascarpone

250ml double cream

150ml whisky

250ml espresso coffee

30 *Savoiardi* sponge fingers (you can always make these Italian 'lady's fingers' biscuits yourself if the fancy takes you!)

Cocoa powder, for dusting

This authentic Italian dessert has been given a Scottish twist by replacing the traditional sweet Marsala wine with whisky. This boozy dessert is perfect for making in advance, with just a final flurry of cocoa powder needed before bringing it to the table.

METHOD

Separate the egg whites and yolks. In a large bowl, whisk the egg yolks and sugar together until pale and creamy. Stir the mascarpone into the egg mixture until well combined.

In another bowl, whip the double cream until soft peaks form. Fold the whipped cream into the mascarpone mixture.

In yet another bowl, whip the egg whites to soft peaks, then fold these lightly into the mascarpone cream mixture.

Mix the whisky and espresso in a shallow bowl. Quickly dip each sponge finger into the bowl for 2 seconds. Layer half the sponge fingers on the bottom of a glass serving dish, then top with half of the mascarpone cream. Repeat the dipped sponge finger layer, topping with the mascarpone cream.

Cover and rest in the fridge for at least 6 hours. Just before serving, dust a generous layer of cocoa powder on the top.

HOT TODDY CHOUX BUNS

(MAKES 16 TO 18)

INGREDIENTS

For the crème pâtissière

250ml milk

3 egg yolks

20g cornflour

1 teaspoon vanilla extract

60g sugar

30ml whisky

1 heaped teaspoon honey

25g butter, cubed

For the choux buns

225ml milk

115g butter

Pinch of salt

140g strong white flour

4 eggs, whisked

For the chocolate topping

200g milk chocolate

This recipe reignites the Auld Alliance of 1295 between Scotland and France. This treaty stipulated that if either country were attacked by the English, the other would invade England. Let's keep this alliance more peaceful by blending the best of French pastry and Scottish flavours. *Chou* is the French for cabbage – and, delightfully, *mon petit chou* can be used to address your sweetheart . . . These wee cabbage-shaped pastry buns are filled with a honey and whisky flavoured crème pâtissière. *Voilà!*

METHOD

To make the crème pâtissière, first warm up your milk in a saucepan.

In a bowl whisk together your egg yolks, cornflour, vanilla, sugar, whisky and honey. Once combined, add a wee bit of the warm milk and stir constantly. Add this back into the saucepan with the rest of the milk and stir until thick. Take off the heat and keep stirring while you add cubes of butter.

To let it chill and set, cover with cling film (pressing down onto the surface of the crème pâtissière), and place in the fridge.

To make the choux buns, first preheat your oven to 200°C/390°F.

Warm the milk, butter and salt in a saucepan. Once the butter has melted, add the flour. This will turn into a dough; keep stirring for 2 minutes to get it smooth. Take off the heat and leave to cool enough that you don't see steam rising from the pan, then slowly add your whisked eggs, stirring all the time. It should make a thick dough that drops off a spoon if shaken.

Place in a piping bag and pipe wee dollops onto a baking tray lined with parchment. Wet your finger and dampen down any points on top of the bun.

Place in the oven for 10 minutes then reduce the temperature to 170°C/340°F for the final 15 minutes. Do not open the oven door! Once you take them out, pierce each of the buns immediately to let the steam out.

To assemble, make a cross on the bottom of each bun. Put your crème pâtissière in a piping bag and fill each bun. Now break up the chocolate, add half to a bowl and place in the microwave in bursts of 20 seconds until melted. Add the rest of the chocolate and stir until fully melted. Dip the top of each bun into the chocolate and leave to set on a rack before serving.

CHOCOLATE, ORANGE & WHISKY MOUSSE

(SERVES 3 TO 4)

INGREDIENTS

150ml double cream

75ml dark chocolate

1 egg

15g sugar

½ tablespoon whisky

½ an orange, zested

Cocoa powder, for dusting

As they say in Gaelic:

Cha deoch-slàinte i gun a tràghadh.

'It's not a toast to good health if the glass isn't emptied.'

There won't be any worries about folk not finishing this mousse. Its classic combination of flavours in a light, airy dessert will definitely have everyone toasting the chef!

METHOD

Warm 75ml of your cream in a saucepan. Once it begins to simmer, take off the heat and add your chocolate which you have roughly chopped into chunks. Stir until melted and leave to cool.

In another bowl whisk the remaining cream until you get soft peaks.

Separate the egg white and yolk. Place the egg white in a large bowl and whisk until firm, add the sugar a teaspoon at a time and whisk until combined. Fold this into the peaks of cream.

In a small bowl add the whisky and orange zest to the egg yolk. Stir into your melted chocolate.

Fold your chocolate into your cream mixture. Spoon into 3 or 4 ramekins – or a cute cup of your choice – and chill in the fridge for at least 4 hours.

Dust with cocoa powder and serve.

JURA TRUFFLES

(MAKES ABOUT 25)

INGREDIENTS

300g dark chocolate

200ml double cream

80g butter

1 teaspoon instant espresso
powder

4 tablespoons Jura whisky

6 tablespoons cocoa
powder

The island of Jura is sixty miles off the west coast of Scotland. Part of
the Inner Hebrides, it has a community of 212 people and one whisky
distillery – I like that ratio! Their whisky works perfectly in this rich truffle
recipe.

METHOD

Roughly chop the chocolate and place in a large bowl.

Add the cream and butter to a saucepan. Once it comes to a boil, pour
over the chocolate and add the espresso powder.

Whisk the chocolate mixture until it starts to thicken (about 5 minutes), then
add the Jura whisky.

When the chocolate is thick enough to hold its shape, spoon into a piping
bag. Pipe the truffles onto a board (you should get about 25), then place in
the fridge to set.

Dust another board with the cocoa powder and roll the truffles so as to
cover them in the powder.

BRAMBLE WHISKY

(MAKES 1 BOTTLE)

INGREDIENTS

350g brambles

2 limes, zested and juiced

50g sugar

500ml whisky

The flavours of brambles and whisky are quintessentially Scottish – together they work perfectly. With a little effort and a lot of patience, you will be gifted with something quite unique. If you cannot pick your own brambles, blackberries will work too.

METHOD

Tip the brambles into a large jar along with the zest and juice of the limes. Gently muddle them before adding the sugar and whisky.

Seal the jar and shake well. Store in a cool, dark cupboard but bring out every day for a month to shake. Then store for at least 2 more months.

Once ready to taste, sieve the whisky through muslin or a clean kitchen towel.

Serve as an after-dinner digestif.

GAELIC COFFEE

(SERVES 1)

INGREDIENTS

1 teaspoon light brown sugar

150ml freshly brewed black coffee

50ml Scottish whisky

2 tablespoons double cream

Pinch of freshly grated nutmeg

So, while the Irish and Americans call it whiskey, Scottish, Canadian and Japanese drinkers call it whisky. The only (but very important) difference between and Irish Coffee and a Gaelic Coffee is where the dram comes from. Make sure that for the Gaelic version you use your favourite Scottish whisky! And always drink through the cream, never stir with a spoon.

METHOD

Fill a glass latte mug with hot water and let it sit for 2 minutes. Pour out the water and add the brown sugar. Pour over hot coffee and stir to dissolve the sugar, then pour in the whisky.

In a separate bowl whisk your cream until soft peaks form. The cream should be thick but still pourable. Gently pour it over the back of a warm spoon to form a thick layer on top of the coffee. Garnish with freshly grated nutmeg and enjoy.

CHOCOLATE STOUT CAKE

INGREDIENTS

For the cake

75g dark chocolate

100g butter

200ml black stout

2 eggs

100g caster sugar

100g soft brown sugar

20g cocoa powder

200g plain flour

1 teaspoon baking powder

For the topping

100g butter, softened

200g icing sugar

100g full-fat cream cheese, at
room temperature

A simple cream cheese frosting blends perfectly with this rich, dense, slightly bitter cake to make it look like an irresistibly well-poured pint of black stout.

METHOD

Preheat the oven to 180°C/350°F. Grease a 23cm cake tin.

Roughly chop the chocolate and butter and place in a saucepan over a low heat. Remove from the heat when melted and leave aside for 5 minutes before stirring in the stout.

In a bowl, use a hand mixer to beat the eggs and sugars together for about 3 minutes.

In another bowl, add the cocoa powder, flour and baking powder.

Now, a third at a time, whisk the egg mixture then the dry ingredients into the stout mixture. Continue until it's all combined.

Pour the batter into your prepared tin and bake for 40 minutes, or until a skewer comes out clean.

Cool in the tin for 5 minutes, then place on a wire rack.

To make the topping, make sure your butter is very soft before sieving in your icing sugar. Beat well together, then blend in the cream cheese.

Layer thickly on top of the cake and serve.

CÈILIDH & KILTS

'Take your partners for an Orcadian Strip the Willow!'

It's 11.50 p.m. on the 31st of December as the cèilidh band caller announces the final dance of the year. My cousin Helen grabs my arm and whisks me off to the dance floor. The accordion player strikes up the tune and the hall is suddenly filled with kilts swishing, couples spinning and folk cheering. I work my way down the line of dancers spinning each in turn as the band plays a set of jigs: 'Atholl Highlanders', 'Caliope House' and 'Jig of Slurs'. Always remembering the golden rule – right hand to your partner, left hand down the line.

It's 11.59 p.m. now. Folk gather, making sure their glasses are filled and their loved ones are close by. The bells begin the countdown to midnight. *'THREE, TWO, ONE!'* The clock strikes twelve.

'Bliadhna Mhath Ùr – Happy New Year!' are the cries we all share as the first drams of the new year are drunk and friends, family and strangers are hugged.

It's five minutes past midnight and the fiddle player slowly begins his tune. Everyone makes a circle, holding hands on the dance floor and solemnly folk begin to sing:

> *Should auld acquaintance be forgot,*
> *And never brought to mind?*
> *Should auld acquaintance be forgot,*
> *And auld lang syne!*

I don't know another tune that can evoke such a sense of belonging, fellowship and nostalgia as 'Auld Lang Syne'. These words of the Rabbie Burns poem talk of preserving old friendships and looking back over the events of the year. New customs and old traditions intertwine at the cèilidh and there's nowhere in the world I'd rather be on Hogmanay.

Cèilidh is simply the Gaelic word for a visit. In years gone by, a cèilidh to another house on the island would have included stories or traditional songs sung by the fire. But now the term is synonymous with a gathering of Scottish dancing. When I have taken friends to their first cèilidh, they always ask, 'How do you know all these dances?' I realise they are hardwired into my brain – and feet! – from being taught them at school. As alongside the obligatory maths, English and history on the curriculum, many hours were spent learning the steps to the 'Dashing White Sergeant', 'Gay Gordons' and 'Highland Schottische'. Looking back, I have used those dancing skills more than those learned in any other class I had!

As the Hogmanay cèilidh comes to an end, another tradition comes to the fore. After midnight, we visit neighbours, family and friends to celebrate the coming of the New Year – a visit in which we 'First Foot' them. If a tall, dark-haired man bearing whisky, black bun and coal as gifts arrives at your doorstep after the bells, it is a sign of good luck for the year ahead. The story goes that it is specifically a dark-haired man who brings luck, as in the days of the Vikings, a burly blond man knocking on your door at midnight might have meant you wouldn't be so fortunate . . .

When I was nineteen, I moved to Russia. I got myself a job in Moscow teaching English to adults. I often think of those twenty or so Russian folk who now speak English with a very strong Hebridean accent and it makes me chuckle. The week before Christmas, I asked each of my students to tell a festive story. Olga

walked to the front of the classroom with a battered old book and a cake. 'I read in my English book that Christmas isn't celebrated in Scotland, so to make up for it, Mr MacLeod, I have baked you Medovik,' she said lifting the cake up, as her fellow students cheered. I sat there baffled. Did she just say that we don't celebrate Christmas in Scotland? I didn't want to spoil the festive mood, so I cheered along with the others, sliced up the layered honey cake and sat drinking vodka and singing songs until class was over.

The next morning, still puzzled by Olga's revelation (and a little fuzzy-headed from the vodka), I began to read about the history of Christmas in Scotland.

The Scots word Yule comes from the Old Norse *Jól*, a midwinter pagan celebration of the winter solstice. With the establishment of the Catholic Church in Scotland in the fifth century, pagan and Christian traditions combined to create a day of feasting and celebration.

After the Reformation of 1560, anti-Catholic sentiment rose. Seeing the holiday as one created by the Catholic Church, John Knox, founder of the Presbyterian Church of Scotland, banned the celebration of Christmas in Scotland. This became enforced by law in the 1640 Act of Scottish Parliament. It wasn't until four hundred years later in 1958 that the 25th of December finally became a Scottish holiday – so, in fact, Olga was absolutely correct. Was this, I wondered, the reason Scotland became so passionate about having a wild night out on New Year's Eve?

While the rest of Scotland spent the 31st of December celebrating Hogmanay, even as late as the 1800s, the Julian calendar was still being used to recognise the coming of the new year in the Hebrides. And so, the 12th of January was New Year's Eve, or in Gaelic *Oidhche Challainn*. Traditionally the day began with the house being cleaned from top to toe,

bedclothes were changed and clothes were mended. Debts were settled, borrowed items were returned. And since nothing should leave the house on New Year's Day, in case the luck should go with it, ashes from the fire were thrown out the night before. The old year was seen out, and the new year welcomed in, with a tidy and ordered household.

That evening, the boys of the village *Gillean Challainn* would gather in the early evening darkness, with their faces hidden by masks. The oldest boy *Ceannard na Callainn* would be wrapped in a sheepskin, often with the horns still on.

Each home in the village would be visited. As they arrived, they would go clockwise around the house three times, striking the walls to ward off evil spirits. As they returned to the front door, they would request entry by reciting a duan – a Gaelic rhyme, which began:

Tha mise nochd a' tighinn gur n-ionnsaigh,
a dh'ùrachadh dhuibh na Callaig.

Tonight I come visiting you, to renew for you the year.

One of the boys would carry a *caisein-uchd*, the breast-strip of a sheep dipped in wax. As they entered, it was lit by the household's fire. This candle would be passed around each family member and would be circled three times around their head. If the flame died, it foretold death or misfortune to the person below.

The reciters of the *duan* would then be rewarded by gifts of freshly baked bannocks, bread, sugar and sweets. It would then be time to leave for the next house, with a blessing on the home left as a parting wish:

Beannaich an taigh 's na tha ann
Eadar choin 's cheit 's chlann
Pailteas bidhe 's pailteas aodaich
'S slàinte dhaoine gun robh ann

Which translates as:

Blessings on this house, and all who enter.
Dogs and cats and children alike.
With food and clothes aplenty.
Good health to all!

Then there was just one more tradition before the clock struck midnight on the 31st of December. Every home would open their back door to let the old year out and then open the front door to welcome the new year in. I will definitely keep up these traditions as Hogmanay comes round each year. *Bliadhna Mhath Ùr!*

8
FESTIVE BAKES

Obhari Obhari, bean an taighe

Thèirig suas 's bheir a-nuas am bonnach mòr

Na geàrr cùl lùdaig

Na geàrr cùl càbaig

Ithidh sinn an t-aran gun an t-ìm

Ithidh sinn an t-ìm gun an t-aran

Ithidh sinn na h-uighean leotha fhèin

Agus carson a-rèist a tha sinn falamh

A' Challainn seo.

Greetings to the woman of the house
Go up and bring out the big scone
Mind how you slice the cheese . . .
Don't just cut the rind!
We will eat bread without butter
We will eat butter without bread
We'll eat eggs on their own
Why are we hungry at this new year?

GRANNY ANNAG'S CHRISTMAS CAKE

INGREDIENTS

For the fruit preparation

310g currants

310g sultanas

200g raisins

85g dried mixed peel

225g glacé cherries

140ml strong black tea

140ml whisky

For the rest of the cake

70g self-raising flour

170g plain flour

1 teaspoon cinnamon

½ teaspoon mixed spice

Pinch of grated nutmeg

200g butter

200g soft brown sugar

1 tablespoon black treacle

1 teaspoon gravy browning
(Vegetarians, leave this
secret ingredient out. Don't
worry, your cake will still
be delicious!)

4 eggs

60g ground almonds

1 orange, zested

1 lemon, zested

Peter's granny was born in Staffin on the Isle of Skye. Famously, after a festive glass of sherry made her cheeks go pink, Granny Annag stayed teetotal for the rest of her life! Her Christmas cake recipe is best made at least 2 months in advance, thus allowing the flavours to mature – with the encouragement of feeding it a dram on a weekly basis. I recommend whisky, but you can use sherry or brandy if you prefer. And wait until you see what Granny Annag's secret ingredient is . . .

METHOD

Firstly, you need to prepare your fruit. Add all the dried fruit, peel and cherries into a large bowl. Pour over your cooled black tea and whisky, cover and rest for 24 hours.

Now you are ready to make the cake. Preheat your oven to 150°C/ 300°F. Line a deep 20cm cake tin with a double layer of baking parchment, then wrap a long strip of folded over newspaper – or brown parcel paper if you prefer – around the outside and tie firmly with string to secure. This helps protect your cake while it's in the oven.

Sieve all your dry ingredients and spices into a bowl. Then, in another bowl, cream your butter and sugar together. Now whisk in your black treacle and Granny Annag's secret ingredient . . . gravy browning!

Next, a bit at a time, whisk in an egg, then a quarter of your dry ingredients and repeat until they are all combined. Finally, pour in your soaked fruit, ground almonds and the zest of the orange and lemon.

Tip your mix into your prepared tin, level the top and bake for 2½ hours. Do the skewer test to make sure it's cooked – a skewer inserted should come out clean. Then let it cool slightly in the tin before turning out to cool fully on a wire rack. Then store wrapped in parchment paper and foil in a sealed tin.

Each week until Christmas, carefully pull back the parchment paper and foil and *feed* the cake, by brushing over a dram of whisky.

A week or so before Christmas, your cake will be ready to decorate. First, gently warm the apricot jam in a pan and brush it all over the cake. Roll the marzipan out to a 3mm thickness – keeping some in reserve for your

To feed the cake

A dram of whisky every
    week!

To decorate the cake

4 tablespoons apricot jam

1kg marzipan

750g fondant icing

3 glacé cherries

1 sprig of holly

'custard' decoration. Use the rolling pin to help you lift the marzipan. Lift it over the cake and carefully unroll. Ease it down the sides, smooth the surface and trim any excess marzipan from the base.

Then roll out and place the fondant icing in a similar fashion over the marzipan. Make it look as smooth and perfect as you can.

Now find a plate 2cm smaller than the diameter of the cake. Place on top of the cake and cut around it. Remove the icing and fondant from beneath.

Cut out the shape of poured custard from your marzipan and place back on top of the cake to give the effect of a Christmas pudding. Add a trio of glacé cherries and a sprig of holly to create the final effect. *Nollaig Chridheil!*

HOT GIN TODDY

(SERVES 2)

INGREDIENTS

300ml water

1 ginger teabag

2 cinnamon sticks

4 cardamom pods

4 whole cloves

1 tablespoon clear honey

1 tablespoon lemon juice

100ml gin

This restorative drink will ward away a cold or fever, but remember prevention is better than cure!

METHOD

Into a saucepan pour your water, a ginger teabag, the cinnamon sticks, cardamom pods and cloves. Simmer. After 5 minutes stir in the honey and lemon juice and leave on the heat for another 5 minutes.

Remove from the heat and add the gin.

Pour into a large mug each and sit together by the fire.

MINCEMEAT OAT COOKIES

INGREDIENTS

For the mincemeat

175g currants

175g raisins

175g sultanas

100g mixed peel

1 cooking apple

125g butter

50g blanched almonds

225g soft brown sugar

½ teaspoon ground
cinnamon

1 teaspoon mixed spice

1 orange, zested and juiced

200ml brandy, rum or sherry

For the cookies

100g butter

50g soft brown sugar

50g plain flour

100g oats

3 tablespoons mincemeat

1 tablespoon maple syrup or
honey

Icing sugar, to dust

No animals were harmed in the making of this mincemeat! Christmas wouldn't be complete without mince pies – but I stumbled upon the idea of using mincemeat in cookies when I found a leftover jar in my cupboard. It's like an oat and raisin cookie taken up a level. But first, let me teach you how to make mincemeat.

METHOD

Measure all of the mincemeat ingredients except the alcohol into a large pan. Heat gently, allowing the butter to melt, then simmer, stirring occasionally, for about 10 minutes.

Allow the mixture to cool completely then stir in the brandy, rum or sherry.

Have 4 sterilised jam jars ready and spoon the mincemeat in. Seal and label. It should keep for at least 6 months.

Now you're ready to make the cookies. First, preheat your oven to 180°C/350°F. Line a baking tray with parchment paper.

In a bowl, cream your butter and sugar together then add your flour. Stir in your oats, then add your homemade mincemeat and maple syrup or honey.

Scoop about 2 tablespoons of the oaty mix into your hands, roll into balls and position them apart on your baking tray.

Place them in the oven for 15 to 18 minutes, put on a wire rack to cool and dust with icing sugar before serving.

TIPSY LAIRD

(MAKES 6 INDIVIDUAL TRIFLES)

INGREDIENTS

500g raspberries

60g sugar

1 lemon, juiced

150ml whisky

12 Savoiardi sponge fingers

400ml chilled vanilla custard
made extra thick
(see page 173)

200ml double cream

25g dark chocolate, grated

Christmas celebrations are not complete without a trifle. Tipsy Laird – aka the Drunk Lord – is a Scottish trifle made using fresh Scottish raspberries and whisky instead of the more commonly used sherry. Make sure you have my custard recipe (see page 173) to hand, but make it extra thick for your trifle by keeping it over the heat for an extra couple of minutes.

METHOD

Put 200g of the raspberries in a saucepan along with the sugar and a tablespoon of lemon juice. Cook on a high heat for a minute. Remove from the heat and, once cooled, mash in another 200g of raspberries.

Take 6 whisky tumblers and place a layer of the raspberry sauce on the bottom of each one.

Pour the whisky into a shallow bowl, turn the sponge fingers over in them twice and then place these on top of the raspberry sauce. Pour the remaining whisky into the leftover raspberry sauce, stir and pour over the sponge fingers. Place in the fridge for 30 minutes.

Add a pair of fresh raspberries to each glass and then pour a thick layer of chilled homemade custard on top.

Keep in the fridge until you are nearly ready to serve.

Then whip the double cream until soft peaks appear then add a generous spoonful or so on top of the custard before adding a final pair of fresh raspberries. Finish by grating some dark chocolate over the top.

PORK & BLACK PUDDING SAUSAGE ROLLS

(MAKES 8)

INGREDIENTS

For the rough puff pastry

175g butter, cold

350g plain flour

Pinch of salt

3–4 tablespoons cold water

1 egg, beaten with a splash of milk to use as a wash

Handful of pumpkin seeds, to top

For the filling

250g black pudding, ideally from Charles MacLeod Butchers in Stornoway!

750g pork sausage meat

1 teaspoon dried thyme

1 teaspoon chopped sage leaves

1 teaspoon salt

1 teaspoon Worcestershire Sauce

Freshly ground black pepper

After a night of cèilidh dancing on Hogmanay, you'll need a pre-prepared post-midnight snack for the revellers. These sausage rolls with black pudding will go down a treat!

METHOD

Cut your butter into cubes and combine with the flour and salt in a bowl. Add water, a tablespoon at a time, until you have a firm dough.

Flour your work surface and roll out the dough into a rectangle that's 1cm thick. Now fold the shorter ends into the middle and give it a quarter turn. Roll again and repeat this 4 more times. Wrap the pastry in cling film, then place in the fridge for an hour.

To make the filling, place all the ingredients, except the black pudding, into a large bowl. Squish it all together with your hands.

On a floured surface, roll out the chilled pastry to a rectangle, roughly 50cm x 15cm and 4mm thick. Spoon the sausage meat onto the long side of the pastry, about 5cm in from the edge, and squeeze it together to make a sausage shape.

Next, cut the black pudding into 1cm sticks and lay these on top of the sausage meat. Brush the pastry edge with your egg wash and fold the other side of the pastry over the top of the filling. Squeeze the edges together to create a sealed join of pastry.

Brush the pastry with the rest of the egg wash, scatter the top with pumpkin seeds, before placing the roll in the fridge to chill for 15 minutes.

Now preheat the oven to 180°C/350°F.

Using a sharp knife, slice the roll into 8 and lay each piece on a lined baking tray. Bake in the oven for 35 to 40 minutes, until golden brown. Remove the sausage rolls from the tray and allow to cool on a wire rack. These are delicious warm or cold!

BLACK BUN

INGREDIENTS

For the pastry

200g plain flour

½ teaspoon baking powder

Pinch of salt

50g vegetable suet

50g butter

4 tablespoons cold water

1 egg, beaten, to glaze

For the filling

200g plain flour

200g raisins

400g currants

1 teaspoon mixed spice

1 teaspoon ground ginger

100g dark muscovado sugar

100g mixed peel

½ teaspoon bicarbonate of soda

1 tablespoon whisky

1 egg

3 tablespoons milk

Black Bun is synonymous with 'first footing', the tradition of bringing gifts to your friends and neighbours after the bells on Hogmanay. Robert Louis Stevenson even talks about these buns in his book, *Picturesque Notes on Edinburgh* written in 1879, in which he says that many stores he walked past displayed them in their windows for sale. Bring good wishes for the year ahead to your neighbours by baking these tasty treats for them.

METHOD

For the pastry, sift the flour, baking powder and salt into a bowl and rub in the suet and butter until the mixture resembles breadcrumbs.

Add the cold water and mix to a soft dough. Turn out and knead into a ball. Cover in cling film and leave to chill in the fridge while you make the filling.

Preheat the oven to 180°C/ 350°F. Line a 900g loaf tin with baking parchment.

Add all the filling ingredients together into a large bowl and combine.

Flour your work surface and roll out two-thirds of the pastry to a rectangle large enough to line the tin. Drape into the tin and press up against the sides. Spoon the filling into the tin and don't leave any spaces.

Roll out the remaining pastry to a rectangle to fit the top. Dampen the edge of the pastry in the tin with a little water, press the pastry lid on top to seal and then trim off the edges.

Glaze with beaten egg and bake for 2 hours. Remove from the oven and leave to cool in the tin before turning out and cutting into slices to serve.

HEBRIDEAN HOGMANAY COCKTAIL

(SERVES 1)

INGREDIENTS

3 tablespoons marmalade
(see page 21 to make
your own)

200ml herbal tea
(choose your favourite!)

1 clementine, juiced

50ml whisky – roughly, a
double dram

5–6 ice cubes, enough to fill
your whisky glass

How do you say Happy New Year in Gaelic? *Bliadhna Mhath Ùr!* This cocktail should bring plenty of Hogmanay cheer – but, remember, it doesn't need to be the 31st of December to drink it. Obviously you can increase quantities to make more of this cocktail to share with your guests.

METHOD

Scoop your marmalade into a large mug. Get the kettle on, then make a cup of your favourite herbal tea and once it's steeped, pour over your marmalade and stir until combined. Let that cool.

Squeeze the juice from the clementine.

To assemble, fill a whisky tumbler with ice, pour in the double dram of whisky, the clementine juice and the cooled marmalade-infused tea. Garnish and serve your Hogmanay guests!

NEW YEAR'S DAY STEAK PIE

INGREDIENTS

500g braising steak

1–2 tablespoons oil

1 onion

2 carrots

2 leeks

2 sticks celery

2 garlic cloves, chopped

2 tablespoons plain flour

1 tablespoon tomato purée

Salt and pepper

Dash of Worcestershire
Sauce

500ml beef stock

375g puff pastry, shop
bought is fine!

1 egg, beaten to use as a
glaze

Having a steak pie on New Year's Day is as much a Scottish tradition as drinking whisky at the Hogmanay cèilidh the night before!

METHOD

Cut the steak into chunks and brown in a large, oiled pan in batches and set aside.

Chop your onion, carrots, leeks and celery, then add the vegetables to the pan with a tablespoon of oil on a low heat and allow 7 to 10 minutes to soften. Add the chopped garlic and flour and stir through.

Then add the tomato purée, salt and pepper, the steak, Worcestershire Sauce and beef stock. Cover and simmer for at least 90 minutes, stirring occasionally until the meat is tender and the stock thickened.

Now preheat the oven to 180°C/350°F.

Spoon the thickened beef stew into a 2-litre pie dish.

Roll out the puff pastry and cut off a long thin strip. Brush this with beaten egg and place all around the outer rim of the pie dish. Lay the rest of the pastry over the dish and trim off any excess. Seal by crimping the edges with a fork. Brush with beaten egg and slice a hole in the top to let the steam escape.

Bake for 30 to 35 minutes, until the pastry is golden. Serve with root vegetables and mashed potatoes – then enjoy a meal guaranteed to get your New Year off to the perfect start!

A BAKING PLAYLIST

There is nothing I enjoy more than a long lazy day baking in the kitchen and music is the perfect complement to that. This is a playlist of Gaelic and Highland tunes I love to bake to. I hope it inspires you to listen to more music from these artists.

The Gentle Light That Wakes Me
Duncan Chisholm

Dh'èirich Mi Moch, B'fheàrr Nach d' Dh'èirich – Julie Fowlis

Gleann Baile Chaoil
Karen Matheson

Tàladh Dhòmhnaill Ghuirm
Kim Carnie

Iain Ghlinn Cuaich
Eilidh Cormack

Òran Chalum Sgàire
Rachel Walker

A Mhairead Nan Cuiread
Joy Dunlop

Walking in the Waves
Skipinnish

Another Scatter!
Trail West

Far Side of the World
Tide Lines

A Mhic Iain 'ic Sheumais
Kathleen MacInnes

Tàladh na Beinne Guirme
MacGregor, Brechin & Ó hEadhra

Thairis Air a' Ghleann
Glasgow Islay Gaelic Choir

Bothan Àirigh am Bràigh Raithneach
Julie Fowlis

Tilidh Mi
Mànran

An Tèid Thu Leam a Mhàiri?
Brian Ó hEadhra & Fionnag NicChoinnich

Cianalas
Jane Hepburn MacMillan & Andy Yearly